Make Mine Vanilla

Lee Edwards Benning

A Fireside Book
Published by Simon & Schuster
New York London Toronto Sydney Tokyo Singapore

FIRESIDE
Simon & Schuster Building
Rockefeller Center
1230 Avenue of the Americas
New York, New York 10020

Designed by Bonni Leon
Manufactured in the United States of America

1   3   5   7   9   10   8   6   4   2

Library of Congress Cataloging in Publication Data

Benning, Lee Edwards, date.
Make mine vanilla/Lee Edwards Benning.
p.   cm.
"A Fireside book."
Includes bibliographical references (p.   ) index.
1. Cookery (Vanilla)   2. Confectionery.   I. Title.
TX819.V35B46   1992
641.6′382—dc20   92-21963
CIP
ISBN: 0-671-73439-3

To Arthur E. Benning,
Senior and Junior,
whose constant refrain has been,
"Make mine vanilla!"

Acknowledgments

They say confession is good for the soul, so here goes: I didn't create all these recipes. Many are part of the standard repertoire; I updated and streamlined them. Others are the result of recipe-sharing by three decades worth of caring friends whose names range from Anna, Barbara, and Cheri on through to Virginia. To you generous souls go my thanks.

To those in the vanilla industry who not only shared expertise but even free product samples, something more tangible than a mere thank you: I've included your firm's name and address in the back of this book so readers can order your products.

Kudos go to all those researchers whose expert services come free with the issuing of a library card, in particular Trudie Buri, Loretta Ryder, and Larry Forry.

I would also be remiss if I didn't acknowledge Jane Jordan Browne's part in finding a home for my manuscript.

Which leaves but one other person whose professionalism and attention to detail equals that of the legendary editors of old. I refer, of course, to Sydny Miner.

Contents

Enhancers 91

Vanilla Ice Cream 103

Introduction

Q: What do you get when a chocoholic and a chocolergic meet,
and wed, and beget?
A: A probable chocolergic with chocoholic tendencies.

And that, twenty-two years ago, was when the fun began. What to serve at birthday parties, what to take to bake sales, what to give as snacks and treats, what to put in Easter baskets, challenged me, the chocoholic in the riddle, time and again. I had to come up with non-chocolate goodies scrumptious enough to satisfy chocoholic and chocolergic alike. Since (according to allergist Harold Lecks of Children's Hospital in Philadelphia) nobody but *nobody* is allergic to vanilla, vanilla recipes became the backbone of my dessert repertoire. One day when I stopped to count them, even I was astonished at how many there were.

A History of Vanilla

We Americans think of chocolate as *the* flavor. Not so the Europeans, especially the master confectioners. For example, as late as 1902, Auguste Escoffier, in his world-famous *Guide Culinaire*, cites 2,973 recipes, only one of which is chocolate—a chocolate sauce. In the 1970s, Gaston Lenotre, who developed La Nouvelle Pâtissière Française (and wrote about it in two volumes), offered 428 recipes with a little over 25 percent requiring vanilla and 25 recipes—total—requiring chocolate.

Although vanilla and chocolate were introduced by Cortés to Europe at the same time, they are flavors of a different kind. Where chocolate is dominating, vanilla is accommodating. The best metaphor I can draw is that chocolate is masculine, while vanilla is more traditionally feminine. Although vanilla has a style all of her own, when necessary she willingly subordinates herself to others in her "life" (read "recipe").

And when Sydney Smith (1771–1845) said of his daughter, Lady Holland, "Ah, you flavor everything; you are the vanilla of society," it was meant, and taken, as the ultimate compliment.

In the beginning, vanilla's role was to enhance chocolate. The first cup of chocolate, given by the Aztec emperor Montezuma II to Hernán Cortés in 1520, was laced with vanilla, which had been sent in tribute to the emperor by the conquered Totonac Indians. Nearly 300 years later, Jean Anthelme Brillat-Savarin, in the definitive *Physiology of Taste* (1825), said, "Chocolate is made by cooking the kernel of the cacao-nut with sugar and cinnamon; such is the classic definition of chocolate . . . [when to that], the delicious flavour of vanilla is added, the *ne plus ultra* of perfection is attained to which this preparation can be brought."

During those 300 years, vanilla had many uses. Early on, it was considered the ultimate aphrodisiac. Not surprising in light of the fact the

Europeans took the word "chocolate" from the Mexican *xocoatl* but discarded vanilla's Mexican name, *tlilxochitl*, or black pod, in favor of the Spanish *vaina*, from the Latin for vagina. And truly the vanilla bean is every Freudian's erotic dream: long and tight, full of seed . . . and when warmed by one's hand (as is done by professional buyers of beans) apt to give off a most intoxicating and inflammatory aroma.

It was this aroma that caused vanilla to be in great demand in perfumery, a natural for an essence variously described as flowery and sharp and tobaccolike . . . pruney and woody and fruity . . . pungent and resinous and sickly sweet. (I remember that during my days at Milwaukee-Downer Seminary we were not allowed to wear cosmetics of any kind. The more adventuresome girls got around this by rubbing geranium petals on their lips and dotting vanilla behind their ears!)

But in the kitchen during the sixteenth century, vanilla's function began and ended in conjunction with chocolate. Interestingly enough, during the seventeenth and eighteenth centuries, it seems to have been the amount of vanilla used that determined the cost of the chocolate. When chocolate became solidified and molded, for example, the cheapest was advertised as containing one-half vanilla bean; the most expensive, two beans. Then at the end of the nineteenth century—in 1878 and 1900—at the Paris Food Expositions, the two Gold Medals awarded to Americans for chocolate manufacture went to Baker's for their Vanilla-Chocolate, made, according to the Walter Baker and Company's promotional literature, "like German

Sweet Chocolate but with the addition of the vanilla bean."

According to one legend, in 1602, Hugh Morgan, apothecary to Elizabeth I, suggested using vanilla as a flavoring by itself. During the following year, the last year of her life, Elizabeth supposedly would only eat and drink foods prepared with vanilla. With such royal patronage, suddenly vanilla was everywhere. At least among those who could afford it: the courts of royalty.

Vanilla proved to be the perfect flavoring. It was suave, smoothing out the harshness of other flavors, such as chocolate and eggs. It was neutralizing, taking the acidity out of lemons and limes. It was supportive, enhancing the richness of fellow ingredients, such as butter and sugar. It was versatile, providing all the flavor by itself or maximizing the flavors of other ingredients: fruits, especially apples, berries, and acidic citrus, and spices such as mace and cinnamon.

It had only one drawback: Vanilla was extraordinarily expensive. When vanilla was first introduced to Europe, sugar was a white treasure, selling for as much as $270 a pound in 1990s dollars; the cost of vanilla has been variously estimated at up to ten times that. The scramble was on to increase the production of vanilla, a scramble almost thwarted by the melipona bee, a native of Mexico and the only insect capable of pollinating the hermaphroditic vanilla plant.

When cuttings were taken to Cuba, England, and France (among other countries), the vanilla plant grew like a real-life version of Jack's beanstalk but produced no beans.

Then in 1807 a vine belonging to the Right Honorable Charles Greville of Paddington, England, not only flowered but fruited as well (a one-time thing, not repeated the following year). The botanical world was agog. Immediately, cuttings were sent all over Europe, including to Antwerp. There, in 1836, a botanist by the name of Charles Morren announced he had solved the mystery and discovered how the plant was pollinated. Edmund Albius, a former slave on the island of Réunion (originally known as the Ile de Bourbon), came up with a practical version of the process, known as the *mariage de vanille*. It consisted of piercing the membrane of the flower with a bamboo skewer to collect the pollen and transferring it to another flower (a method known and used by the Totonacs hundreds of years before). When word got out to the general public, it reinforced vanilla's reputation as an aphrodisiac, which naturally increased the demand for the beans.

The perspicacious saw fortunes to be made. Soon every island with a seemingly suitable climate saw the planting of vanilla plantations. Unfortunately, not all had the warm, moist climate, the regular rainfall, the humus-rich soil, the gently sloping land, that the vine requires.

The vanilla plant is first cousin to the orchid, and the only one of more than 20,000 orchid plants that is edible. Its botanical name comes from the genus *Vanilla* of the family Orchidaceae. For many years, it was identified as *Vanilla planifolia*—and still is—although it was reclassified some years ago to the more appropriate *Vanilla fragrans*.

When commercially cultured, the vine must be espaliered on "tutor" trees, pruned to stay short, in a series of long loops to keep the blooms within reach of workers. From its initial propagation by cutting to the first flowering takes three years. Then one morning the tree is dotted with blooms, small star-shaped orchids, ranging from greenish white to pale yellow, with five long, narrow petals surrounding the crinkle-edged trumpet. If not pollinated, by afternoon the orchid begins to wilt . . . and by nightfall is dead. In the morning, the process begins again. And so it goes for up to two months. The vine must be visited daily, and the blooms hand-pollinated by Albius's 150-year-old process.

During those two months, only between 50 and 150 of the best flowers, depending on the size of the vine, will be hand-pollinated. Too few and the vine doesn't make money. Too many and the vine will be exhausted and die. If the wrong flowers are chosen, the beans will not grow plump and long. Take too long choosing and the blooms will begin dying on you. A skilled laborer can do between 1,500 and 2,000 blooms a day.

But the handwork has only just begun. From pollination to bundling for shipping, everything must be done by hand, making the production of vanilla almost as labor-intensive as that of saffron.

Shortly after pollination come the slender green pods, much like string beans, ranging from four to twelve inches in length and growing in bananalike clusters. Like a human infant, the pod takes its time maturing: from six to nine months. Finally, in late summer, the pods begin to turn yellow at the blossom end or lower tip, indicating that they are ready for gathering (the yellower the bean, the more flavorful the final extract). But as with the flowers, the pods do not all mature at the same time, not even in the same cluster, so each plant must be gone over daily. With some species, if a pod is missed or allowed to ripen naturally, it splits open and can't be sold whole but instead will be used for extract.

Before they can be cured, the pods must be "killed" by either blanching for twenty seconds in hot but not boiling water or roasting in a slow oven. Then, in a fermenting process that can take up to three months, the beans are alternately steamed and sweated by night and dried in the hot sun by day.

Finally, the beans are spread on ventilated stacks in a storehouse for several months to complete the curing and drying. Just before shipping, the beans are sorted, with the biggest and best saved to be sold whole, the rest to be used for vanilla extract.

Ingredients and Other Technicalities

Vanilla, the Bean

The three types of vanilla beans readily available today are

Mexican: From an area near Veracruz, the oldest and the scarcest type and considered the best by most

Bourbon: From the West Indian island of Réunion, and Madagascar, from the island of the same name off the coast of Africa, which are usually treated (even hyphenated) as one type, although the general consensus is that Réunion vanilla is sweeter and spicier while Madagascan is smoother and richer

Tahitian: From the South Pacific island, the youngest of the three and, although looked down on by food snobs, by far the most aromatic

The Mexican bean is thick and a dark, dark brown with streaks of light. It resists bending but is flexible. The Bourbon-Madagascar bean is thinner, darker with reddish streaks, and bends quite easily. The Tahitian is twice the width of the Mexican, a solid dark brown—almost black—plump and bending. It is also slightly shorter than the other two. What amazes me is that if you smell any of the beans, none smells vanilla-y. In fact, the Tahitian has a tobaccolike smell. But touch them and then smell your fingers. Voilà, *vanilla!*

Which is best? Most experts in the vanilla business rank them in the order above. As for myself, I am ambivalent. I keep on hand all three types of beans, as well as their extracts, and I find myself using different vanillas for different purposes. For example, I prefer Tahitian wherever fragrance is a consideration, as in Vanilla-Sugar (see page 141), but would not use it to make Vanilla-Rum (see page 133), since it would overpower the rum. For French vanilla ice cream, on the other hand, I would willingly pay the premium for Mexican beans.

Vanilla beans are graded, and the top grades of the worst beans are preferable to the worst grades of the best beans. For example, according to Waverley Root, the best grade is what the French call "fine vanilla," which is equivalent to the English "legitimate vanilla." Pods are thin, eight to twelve inches long, and almost dead black, with a shiny surface covered with *givre* (French for frost), which is formed by concentrated crystals of vanillin. Sometimes the crystals are obvious, other times, they give the bean a fuzzy look.

Next best is the "woody vanilla" (French) or "bastard vanilla" (English). These pods are five to eight inches long and reddish-brown, with a dull surface.

Coming in third or last is "vanillon" (both French and English) with thick, flattened, short (four to five inches) brown pods.

So how do you find the top grades? You buy from a top source. Avoid those withered things you find in spice bottles in supermarkets and most of what is sold in gourmet stores. To get the best, go mail order; you'll find a list of sources on page 185. I have tried them all and have yet to get a clinker.

There are two schools of thought (both from dealers in beans) on storing vanilla beans: One recommends that the beans be kept in an airtight jar (an apothecary jar with a ground-glass top would be best) in a dark place. Another suggests that the beans be kept in a Ziploc bag, along with a moistened piece of paper towel, and stored in the refrigerator.

I have tried both, but since I use my vanilla beans so prodigiously, they don't have a chance to dry out however they're stored; on the other hand, the beans in the supermarket are so desiccated, I must conclude that an airtight jar won't work miracles.

Vanilla, the Extract

Vanilla extract is the much more convenient, liquid form of vanilla beans and the preference of most Americans.

The extraction of vanillin from the beans is quite similar to perking a pot of coffee: A large stainless steel basket of chopped beans is lowered into a lukewarm blend of alcohol and water, and the mixture is pumped through the chopped beans over and over again.

Because beans vary from lot to lot, the newly perked extract is tested and blended with other batches to make a uniform flavoring. It is then aged, like wine, for several months. During aging, the flavor becomes fuller and softer. Sometimes the aging takes place at the factory. Other times, makers take advantage of the normal time-lag built into our distribution system. In the bottle, aging can continue for two to three years, so never retire your vanilla as too old.

By law, **vanilla extract** must be made with at least 13.5 ounces of vanilla beans to each gallon of liquid and must contain at least 35 percent alcohol. (Stronger concentrations—double and triple strengths, known as twofold and threefold—are used by professional bakers and are available through mail order. Their only advantage is that they take up less storage space.)

Vanilla flavoring contains less alcohol and has a less-concentrated flavor . . . and I can't for the life of me figure any use for it.

Vanilla-vanillin extract, which I understand is available in some parts of the country (but which I've never seen), contains as much as 1 ounce of synthetic vanillin per gallon of liquid and is 35 percent alcohol. Again, I see no use for it except as a money-making ploy on some manufacturer's part.

As with vanilla beans, once you get out of the supermarket and into mail order, it is possible to get extracts of specific beans: Tahitian, Madagascar, even Mexican.

Those who have a preference for a specific type of bean usually prefer the extract of the same bean. Again I choose the bean extract that best suits the recipe. For example, I prefer the Tahitian extract where color is a factor. A lighter brown than its counterparts, I would choose it for white

21

vanilla ice cream, Windtortes, or angel food cakes. I use darker Madagascar for egg custards or anywhere that a more robust flavor is intended. I reserve Mexican for special dishes and celebrations. Speaking of which, there is one more vanilla extract you should know about:

Vanilla essence, available from but one source (see page 188), is made like a French perfume. It is distilled into a concentration so strong that one measures it by the drop. How good is it? Jennifer Lang, in her book *Tastings—The Best from Ketchup to Caviar* (Crown, 1986), writes: "The best vanilla in our tasting—La Cuisine vanilla, called an *essence*, which costs almost five times as much as the other brands in the tasting, but is easily five times better."

I agree it's marvelous: rich, rich, rich, vanilla-y. I recommend it heartily and use it in my own personal cooking life. I did not, however, use it in testing any of the recipes in this book because it is not in general distribution.

Vanilla, the Imitation

Unfortunately, the demand for vanilla beans and pure vanilla extract exceeds supply and has for centuries. There is not, for example, enough natural vanilla to supply the United States alone. In 1876, the first vanilla substitute was developed in Germany from eugenol, which was in turn derived from the essence of clove (the likely reason vanilla was once touted as a home remedy for toothache).

Cloves aren't cheap either. And so the search was on for other sources of vanillin, the characteristic vanilla fragrance. From our paper-making industry came coniferin and lignin, both sources of vanillin. From Mexico, original source of vanilla, came a more dangerous substitute: the tonka bean, which yields coumarin.

Unfortunately coumarin can be toxic, and so, in 1954, extract with coumarin was banned from this country by the U.S. Food and Drug Administration. Extract with coumarin can still be found in Mexico, so be wary of it. In fact, be wary of *any* bargain vanilla. Friends of ours were sent a bottle from Costa Rica that smelled good, but when used, ruined the food . . . maybe luckily for those intended to eat it.

Imitation vanilla is a clear liquid, readily available in this country, and used widely throughout the food industry. It is made from vanillin and/or ethyl vanillin, a coal tar derivative. Its advantages are its strength—three times as vanilla-y as natural—its cost, which is about one-third the cost of real vanilla, and its colorlessness, which makes it a natural for white foods such as cheap vanilla ice cream and angel food cake.

I do not recommend imitation vanilla.

Other Vanilla Ingredients

You'll find Vanilla-Rum and Vanilla-Sugar specified for recipes throughout this book. I'm talking homemade here; you'll find directions on pages 133 and 141.

Other than vanilla beans, I have tried to use no product or ingredient that isn't readily available in the supermarket. And in the case of vanilla beans, if you don't have them, simply substitute vanilla extract (which I refer to throughout simply as vanilla). The rule of thumb is: 1 teaspoon vanilla extract for a 2-inch piece of vanilla bean. When baking, add the vanilla extract when you cream the butter or add the eggs. For cooked custards, add the vanilla after cooling the mixture but before it sets.

Homemade Vanilla Extract

Some people prefer to make their extract with vodka, others with brandy, and I've even heard of some using gin. I find the vodka okay, brandy a waste of money (because you really should use good stuff), and the gin terrible! I prefer light rum. It's mellower, smoother, and much cheaper.

Drop one 8-inch or longer vanilla bean into 1 cup of rum in an airtight jar. Let sit in a cool, dark place for two weeks or more. Add more rum as you use it, and another vanilla bean when the color grows weak.

Other Ingredients

Butter: I am no unsalted butter snob. I have never bought rancid salted butter in a supermarket, although I have bought unsalted with an off taste.

If you use butter sparingly or infrequently, buy salted; it will keep longer. If you are trying to control your salt intake, buy unsalted.

I used salted grade AA butter for all the recipes in this book. Which brings up the question of butter versus margarine: I use butter in anything delicately or butter flavored, since I think you can taste the difference; if you prefer margarine or butter-flavored shortening, be my guest. (I recommend corn oil margarine for the taste and the stick form for ease of measurement.) If you're using shortening, be sure to measure it by the displacement method: Subtract the amount of shortening called for from 8 ounces or 1 cup. Fill a measuring cup with that amount of water. (For example, if you need ⅓ cup shortening, subtract ⅓ cup from 1 cup, which is ⅔ cup. Put ⅔ cup of water in the measuring cup.) Then, add the shortening until you reach the 1-cup mark. Drain well and proceed with the recipe.

Salt: Since I begin with the premise that you will be using salted butter, most of these recipes call for little salt. You may wish to add more or, in some cases, omit the salt called for. The one exception: Don't eliminate the salt when yeast is an ingredient. The salt is necessary to regulate the action of the active bacteria.

Flour: I am driven crazy by cookbooks that don't specify cake, bread, or all-purpose flour; you'll find all of mine do. In some cases, a recipe calls for all-purpose flour and cake flour, to dilute the gluten in all-purpose flour and make a more delicate crumb. Only one recipe calls for self-rising flour.

As a rule, I find sifting flour unnecessary. All-purpose flour is measured by the stir, scoop, and level method. All cake flour can be measured the same way if you keep it in a canister. If not, measure the cake flour by spooning into the cup and then leveling.

Sugar: I always specify whether granulated (meaning regular), superfine (sometimes called instant dissolving, extra fine, or bar sugar), or confectioners' (also known as 10X and powdered) sugar should be used. If you're out of confectioners' sugar and own a blender, you can make your own by putting granulated sugar (dry) into the blender and whirring until it's pulverized. However, you should be aware that commercial confectioners' sugar contains cornstarch, which keeps it from caking and works as a thickener in some recipes.

Eggs: I use extra-large or large eggs, whichever is the better buy (if there's less than seven cents difference per dozen between them, the bigger is the better buy). Also, I do not agree that eggs are easier to separate cold; I find it just the opposite. I *do* agree that warm whites beat higher.

As of the writing of this book, salmonella has become a concern in recipes using uncooked eggs. Wherever possible I have used recipes calling for cooked, rather than uncooked, egg yolks. Those using uncooked eggs generally call for long beating times in which the friction serves to partially cook the egg.

Equipment

Next to an autobiography, I can think of no other type of writing that is more revealing than a cookbook. The very selection of the recipes tells you much about the writer as a person. Do they do things by the book? Do they take shortcuts? Do they like long, convoluted recipes or do they prefer two, three, and four-ingredient quickies? In other words, how much is the author like you? (The more alike you are, the happier you are apt to be with the cookbook.) So, let me save you some guesswork and tell you up front:

My kitchen is not one of those stainless steel showplaces one sees in magazines. My refrigerator and freezer could star in one of those ads touting the durability of a particular brand: They are older than my grown-up son. I have a double oven, but only the top is self-cleaning and the bottom has no broiler. My three concessions to professional cooking are my electric six-burner range top, the marble candy slab my husband bought through the classifieds, and a butcher block obtained the same way.

The three appliances I use the most do not, despite teasing to the contrary, include a can opener. I do have and use a food processor, an electric mixer, and a microwave oven, but none is a commercial size or professional model. (In fact, I have just had to replace my thirty-year-old mixer and, although I bought a famous brand, I like the old one better.)

My one concession to gadgetry is electric ice cream makers: I own four. I have just bought still another in my search for the perfect ice cream machine.

In other words, basically, I cooked all of these recipes in a kitchen no better equipped than yours.

About the Recipes

People ask me where I find my recipes, especially the vanilla ones. Actually, it is not so much a case of *finding them* but of *deciding among them*.

For *Make Mine Vanilla* I could have concentrated on the world's classics and come up with more than a hundred, but didn't. Instead I chose only the most famous or the most basic or the most interesting to make and taste. To these, I added many given to me by friends.

You will find what might appear to be a strange combination of recipes in this book: labor-intensive classics alongside genuine quickies, but none require any great amount of expertise and they should be within the grasp of even a beginning cook. Why? I like to cook, but I have no more time than any other working woman; when I cook, I want either something that goes together fast and tastes better than anything I could buy, or something so spectacular or family-pleasing that I don't mind spending the time.

I believe in shortcuts (I've included tips for nearly every recipe to make life just a bit easier for you), and yes, I use mixes.

All that said, let's get down to cooking.

The Classics

It may have been an Englishman (either Queen Elizabeth I's apothecary or her chef—legends differ) who decided to try vanilla as a flavoring, not just as an adjunct to chocolate, but it was the French who embraced vanilla and took it to their hearts. But they weren't the only ones. The Austrians and the Viennese, the Italians, and the Spaniards—all found in vanilla the perfect flavoring.

You'll find many of their classic desserts here. Each revised to reflect available ingredients and to utilize modern equipment.

Apples Mary Stuart

Supposedly the ill-fated Mary, Queen of Scots, was enamored of this dish as a child. If you like apple pie, you will adore this dish.

Serves 6

6 apples (Rome, Granny Smith, or Yellow Delicious all hold their shape well)
2 cups granulated sugar
3 cups water
One 2-inch piece of vanilla bean or 1 teaspoon vanilla
1 cup Crème Pâtissière Vanillée (page 45)

1 recipe Puff Pastry (page 64), chilled, or 1 package of two frozen puff pastry sheets, thawed and chilled
1 egg, beaten lightly with 1 teaspoon water
Confectioners' sugar

Peel and core the apples; don't cut all the way through to the bottom. Put the sugar, water, and vanilla bean (slice lengthwise and scrape the seeds into the water) into a stockpot or large skillet big enough to hold all 6 apples. Bring to a boil and cook, stirring occasionally, until the sugar dissolves. Stand the apples in the syrup and cover with a lid or an aluminum foil tent. Poach the apples for 15 to 25 minutes, depending on their size, until tender but not too soft. Drain them upside down on a cloth until cool.

Preheat the oven to 375°F. Fill the center of each apple with Crème Pâtissière Vanillée. Roll out the chilled Puff Pastry dough and cut into 6 squares at least twice the height of the apples. Place an apple in the center of each square, and holding the corners with your fingertips, bring them together to form a pouch. Leave the sides partially open to serve as vents. Cut off the excess dough with a scissors. Finish off with a round of pastry cut with a fluted pastry cutter or cookie cutter. Brush the *top only* with the egg wash. Transfer the apples with a spatula to an ungreased cookie sheet. Chill for 30 minutes or more before baking. Bake for 10 to 15 minutes or until the pastry is brown. Sprinkle with confectioners' sugar.

TIPS *Instead of using your apple corer to remove the core, use a pointed teaspoon or grapefruit spoon. Makes the opening more generous.*

To cut the puff pastry, dip a knife in flour and press down, rocking the knife back and forth. Don't drag the knife through the dough, it will stretch it. Handle the cut edges as little as possible.

Austrian Custard Sauce

This just may be the lightest and best custard sauce I've ever had. The end result is very much like a syllabub in texture and lightness. The secret of the sauce is in the beating so that it remains light and fluffy while it cools. This sauce is marvelous when poured over the French Oeufs à la Neige (page 59). If you do this, strain the milk used for the "eggs'" poaching liquid in that recipe and add enough to make the 1¾ cups needed here.

Makes 2 cups

1¾ cups milk
2 whole eggs
2 egg yolks

½ cup granulated sugar
One 2-inch piece of vanilla bean or
    1 teaspoon vanilla

Place all the ingredients (except the vanilla extract, if using) in a 3-quart saucepan. Stirring constantly, bring to a boil over high heat. As soon as the mixture boils, begin beating immediately with a hand-held electric mixer or a wire whip and beat until the mixture is light and frothy. Remove from the heat and continue beating for 5 to 10 minutes while the eggs continue cooking off the heat. The mixture will gradually thicken and rise to within 1 inch of the top of the saucepan. Let cool and remove the vanilla bean or add ½ teaspoon vanilla extract, if using.

TIP   *The higher the heat, the faster you must beat.*

Basic Vanilla Cake

Licking the mixing bowl clean isn't unusual in our house, but when I serve this cake, people have clamored for the chance to clean up the cake pan when the last piece is gone—the cake is that moist and light and delicious . . . even days after making it.

You can make it as fast as any packaged mix, but the results are twice as good. This is a good place to use Tahitian vanilla; it definitely makes for a white cake.

Serves 8 to 12

6 tablespoons butter or ¼ cup
   shortening and 2 tablespoons
   butter, at room temperature
1 cup granulated sugar
1½ teaspoons vanilla

1 teaspoon baking powder
1½ cups cake flour, stirred, scooped,
   and leveled
½ cup milk
2 eggs, beaten

Preheat the oven to 350°F. Grease and flour two 8-inch layer pans.

Cream the butter with the sugar and vanilla. Stir the baking powder into the flour. Add the mixture alternately with the milk, stirring after each addition and ending with the flour. Add the beaten eggs and mix thoroughly. Pour the mixture equally into the pans. Bake for 20 to 25 minutes or until a cake tester comes out clean. Allow to cool for 15 minutes in the pans, then turn onto a rack. Frost with One-Minute Buttercream Frosting (page 179) or serve topped with fruit.

TIP *When alternating dry and wet ingredients, divide the dry ingredients into thirds, the wet ingredients into halves, then start and end with the dry.*

VARIATION

Quick Coffee Cake *Grease and flour an 11-by-8-inch baking pan. Prepare the recipe as above and pour into the pan. Mix 1 teaspoon cinnamon and ¼ cup granulated Vanilla-Sugar (page 141) together and sprinkle over the batter. Scatter ¼ cup walnuts or pecans on top. Dot the top with an additional 4 to 6 tablespoons of chilled butter cut into small pieces. Bake for 30 to 35 minutes or until a cake tester barely comes out clean. The cake should be soft and moist. Cool in the pan.*

TIP *Chill the butter in the freezer, peel the wrapper down as if it were a banana, and use a serrated blade to shave off pieces.*

Cream Puffs and Eclairs (Pâte à Choux)

I absolutely adore these delicate confections, but they've got to be home-made. Cream puffs and eclairs are just too "eggy" for many people's taste; for them, I suggest the addition of vanilla to the basic dough. It won't be noticeable, but it will mute much of the egg taste. Adding milk is not traditional; I borrowed the idea from Judy Gorman, author of *The Culinary Craft* (Yankee Books, 1984). It improves the color of the puffs.

Makes 12 large, 16 medium, or 24 small cream puffs or 8 large or 12 medium eclairs

PÂTE À CHOUX

½ cup butter
¾ cup water
¼ cup milk
2 teaspoons superfine sugar

1 cup all-purpose flour, stirred, scooped, and leveled
4 large eggs
1½ teaspoons vanilla (optional)

Put the butter, water, milk, and sugar in a large saucepan and bring to a boil over medium-high heat. When the butter has completely melted, dump in all the flour all at once and stir hard until the mixture forms a smooth ball that leaves the sides of the pan.

Remove from the heat and allow to cool slightly. Beat in the eggs one by one. The dough will appear slimy at first, then become silky as each egg is incorporated. Beat in the vanilla, if desired. If the dough is stiff—if it doesn't fall lightly from the spoon when lifted—break another egg, beat lightly, and add one-half at a time.

I know it's traditional to make this by hand, or should I say, by wooden spoon. I don't. I transfer the dough from the hot saucepan to the metal bowl of my mixer—which immediately cools it down—then let the mixer do my beating. If your mixing bowl isn't metal or heatproof, use a portable mixer.

CREAM PUFFS

Preheat the oven to 425°F. Using either a pastry bag with a plain tip or a tablespoon, form the puffs on a greased cookie sheet. Using the back of the spoon, flatten any points. Bake for 15 minutes or until golden brown. Turn the oven temperature down to 375°F. Remove the puffs from the oven and immediately stick a knife into the side of each puff. Return the puffs to the oven and bake for 20 minutes more. Place on a rack and let cool completely. Cut the tops off and fill the puffs with Crème Chantilly (page 43) or Crème Pâtissière Vanillée (page 45). Replace each top slightly tilted as if to resemble a cocked hat and serve.

TIP *To make these really glow, you can brush the tops (not the sides) with a glaze made of 1 egg yolk and 1 tablespoon water. The puffs can also be filled with ice cream and frozen. Serve with chocolate sauce.*

ECLAIRS

Preheat the oven to 425°F. Line a cookie sheet with parchment paper or grease it.

Using a pastry bag with a plain tip, pipe the dough into 8 thick sausage or 12 cigar shapes. Using the back of a spoon, round them off. Bake for 20 minutes or until golden brown. Turn the oven temperature down to 375°F. Remove from the oven and immediately stick the point of a knife, 1 inch deep, into each end of the eclairs. Return to the oven and bake for 20 minutes more. Place on a rack and let cool. Cut off the tops. Traditionally, eclairs are filled with Crème Pâtissière Vanillée (page 45) and covered with a chocolate glaze: Melt 1 12-ounce bag semisweet chocolate chips with 1 tablespoon solid shortening.

TIP *To make your eclairs uniform in size, draw 2 parallel lines 3 or more inches apart in dark ink on the underside of the parchment paper. You'll be able to see the lines through the paper.*

Crema Española

This is also known as Spanish Snow and is a type of Bavarian cream. It is, in its simplest form, a cooked, custard-based, gelatin mousse that's molded and served cold.

Serves 4 to 6

One 2-inch piece of vanilla bean or
  1 teaspoon vanilla
2 cups milk
1 envelope unflavored gelatin

¼ cup cold water
3 eggs, separated
⅓ cup granulated sugar
¼ teaspoon salt

In a small saucepan, soak the vanilla bean in the milk for 20 minutes. Then heat the milk until bubbles form around the edge. Keep the milk hot while you continue the recipe.

Sprinkle the gelatin on the cold water and let soften. In a large bowl of an electric mixer, beat the egg yolks with the sugar and salt until well blended. While still beating, very slowly add the hot milk but not the vanilla bean. Transfer the mixture to a saucepan or the top of a double boiler and cook until it thickens but barely coats a spoon. Remove from the heat immediately, and pour back into the mixing bowl. Add the gelatin, mix well, and let cool. If using vanilla extract, add it now. Chill. When the mixture begins to jell (it will jiggle), beat the egg whites until stiff and fold into the mixture.

Pour the *crema* into individual molds or a 1½-quart mold and chill until set, at least 3 hours or overnight. Turn out of the molds and serve with cream or crushed fruit.

TIP *Before filling the mold, grease with a flavorless oil or cooking spray, like Pam; it will make unmolding easier.*

VARIATIONS

Bavarois à la Crème *Proceed as above but instead of using egg whites, fold in 8 ounces of heavy cream, whipped just until stiff.*

Alternate flavors *You can add 3 tablespoons cocoa or 2 teaspoons instant coffee granules to the hot milk. Some chopped pistachios, almonds, or even crushed praline can be folded in after the egg whites or whipped cream, but before chilling.*

Crème Anglaise

This is your basic custard sauce: Add cornstarch (or flour or potato starch) to it and you have Crème Pâtissière Vanillée (page 45). Use it warm over hot gingerbread or, cooled, over cold mousses. Use in a strawberry shortcake instead of whipped cream, and you've got a form of zuppa Inglese.

Makes 2 cups

6 egg yolks
⅔ cup granulated sugar
2 cups milk

½ vanilla bean, split lengthwise,
or 2 teaspoons vanilla

With an electric mixer, beat the egg yolks with the granulated sugar (and vanilla extract if that's what you're using) until thick and lemon colored. In a 3-quart saucepan over medium-high heat, bring the milk and vanilla bean to a slow boil, stirring frequently to prevent scorching. With the mixer running, slowly pour the hot milk through a strainer into the egg yolk mixture, blending well. (Save the vanilla bean for another purpose.) Return the egg yolk–milk mixture to the saucepan. Over medium heat, stirring constantly, cook until the mixture thickens and coats a spoon. *Do not let the mixture come to a boil.* For a truly silky sauce, pour the sauce through a strainer into a bowl to cool. Refrigerate.

TIP   *If you've been saving egg yolks in the refrigerator, pour off any liquid* and use a wooden spoon to scoop out the egg yolks. If they're broken, measure 1 tablespoon plus 1 teaspoon of broken yolk per whole yolk needed.

VARIATION
Chocolate Crème Anglaise   *Instead of using a vanilla bean, add 2 table-spoons crème de cacao and ½ teaspoon vanilla after the custard has cooked.*

Crème Brûlée

One taste and you'll understand why this is a classic vanilla dish! The smooth custard makes a great contrast with the crunchy caramel on top. This should be made the day before serving, but once the caramel top is broken, the custard does not keep that well appearancewise, since the caramel gets runny.

Serves 6

4 egg yolks, well beaten
⅓ cup granulated sugar
2 cups heavy cream
2 teaspoons vanilla, preferably
   Tahitian

1¼ cups soft, firmly packed or
   granulated light-brown sugar

Butter a shallow 9-inch ovenproof pie plate or 6 individual ramekins.

Beat the egg yolks with the sugar with an electric mixer until well combined. Scald the cream, stirring frequently, in a large saucepan. When bubbles appear around the edge, remove from the heat, and, while running the mixer, very slowly dribble about one-quarter of the cream into the egg yolk–sugar mixture. Add the egg yolk mixture to the cream in the saucepan and cook over medium-high heat, stirring constantly, for about 10 minutes, or until the mixture thickens and coats a spoon. Let cool for 10 minutes, then add the vanilla. Pour through a sieve into the prepared pie plate or ramekins. When completely cool, refrigerate and chill at least 3 hours or overnight.

Preheat the broiler. Fill a larger pan with ½ inch ice water. Top the custard with a thin layer (¼–⅓ inch thick, no more) of brown sugar; you should not be able to see the surface of the custard. Place the baking dish(es) in the pan of ice water and run under the broiler for 2 to 3 minutes, leaving the oven door open so you can watch it. The sugar should become very bubbly and caramelize to a darker brown. Don't let it scorch! Allow to cool in the water, remove from the bath, then chill again.

TIPS *If you're serving the custard in one large dish: When ready to serve, tap the caramel gently with a spoon to crack the surface and outline each serving. Serve with a handful of fresh unsweetened strawberries as a garnish.*

If you stir with a wooden spoon, the grain of the wood will not show through when the custard thickens.

Crème Chantilly

You may know this as sweetened whipped cream. Exactly how sweet it is, is up to you; err on the light side, then taste-test. The cornstarch in the confectioners' sugar helps stabilize the cream, which means you can make it a couple of hours in advance.

Makes 2 cups

1 cup heavy cream	2 to 4 tablespoons Vanilla-Sugar (page 141) or 2 to 4 tablespoons confectioners' sugar plus 1 teaspoon vanilla

Chill the small bowl and beaters of an electric mixer.

Beat the heavy cream until it begins to thicken. Add the Vanilla-Sugar. Continue beating, watching closely, until the cream begins to draw away from the bowl. The cream is done when it draws in on itself and the mixer trails are well defined.

TIPS   *If your idea of "in advance" means the night before, put the whipped cream in a cheesecloth-lined colander or strainer over a bowl so any liquid drains off. If you've underbeaten the cream, you can always beat some more, providing you rechill the beaters and bowl.*

For a fast chill, put the bowl and beaters in the ice cube bin of your freezer.

Crème Frite
(Fried Custard)

Yes, fried custard. It was a popular dessert some two decades ago; it's time it was rediscovered. Once made and chilled, the custard is handled like a croquette: dipped in flour and eggs and soft bread crumbs, then fried.

Serves 6

2 whole eggs
½ cup granulated sugar
½ cup rice flour
1 cup milk
1 teaspoon vanilla
All-purpose flour for breading

2 eggs, beaten
Soft white bread crumbs
Butter and mild vegetable oil
 for frying
Vanilla-Sugar (page 141),
 if you have it

Butter and flour a jelly roll pan.

Beat the 2 whole eggs and sugar until fluffy. Add the rice flour, milk, and vanilla. Place the mixture in a 1½-quart saucepan and bring to a boil, cooking until the mixture thickens to the consistency of paste. Spread the mixture about ½ inch thick on the jelly roll pan and chill.

Cut the custard into small diamond-shaped pieces. Dip each piece first into the flour, then into the beaten eggs, and finally into the soft white bread crumbs. Traditionally, these are fried in very hot deep fat, but I prefer to sauté them in butter. In a heavy-bottomed frying pan over medium heat, heat 3 tablespoons of butter and 3 tablespoons of mild vegetable oil. Sauté the custard pieces, being careful not to crowd the pan, until they are browned on one side. Gently turn them over and sauté until they are browned on the other side and warmed through. Drain on paper towels.

Just before serving, sprinkle with Vanilla-Sugar.

TIP *If you can't get rice flour at a local health food store, substitute Cream of Rice. The texture won't be quite as fine, but the end result will be delicious.*

Crème Pâtissière Vanillée

This is the pastry cream used for such highfalutin' desserts as Gâteau Saint-Honoré and Napoleons (page 54). It is equally at home inside Cream Puffs and Eclairs (page 35) and is the custard to use between cake layers. The French make it with flour; I use cornstarch, which speeds up the process. It also adds to the keeping power of the cream.

Makes 2 cups

6 egg yolks

⅔ cup granulated sugar

6 tablespoons cornstarch

2 cups milk

½ vanilla bean, split lengthwise,
 or 2 teaspoons vanilla

With an electric mixer, beat the egg yolks and sugar (and vanilla extract, if using) until thick and lemon colored. Add the cornstarch and mix well. In a 3-quart saucepan over medium-high heat, bring the milk and vanilla bean to a boil, stirring frequently to prevent scorching. With the mixer running, slowly pour the hot milk through a strainer into the egg yolk mixture; mix well. Return the egg yolk–milk mixture to the saucepan. Over medium-high heat, stirring constantly with a whisk, bring the mixture to a boil. It will begin thickening at the bottom; you'll feel some resistance as you stir, then lumps will develop. Keep stirring faster, but don't remove from the heat until the entire mixture begins to come together; it should take less than a minute. Beat with the whisk until smooth. Pour into a clean bowl and chill.

TIP *To keep a skin from forming on the custard, just barely rub the top surface with a stick of butter or dust lightly with confectioners' sugar. Once the mixture has cooled, if you're not going to use right away, press plastic wrap down on the surface to keep the custard from drying out in the refrigerator.*

Croquembouche

This impressive dessert is a pyramid of small custard-filled Cream Puffs glued together with caramel. This is a beauty to see, but somewhat hellish to serve. You will need two spoons to break up the caramel.

Serves 8 to 12

1 cup granulated sugar
¾ cup water
⅓ teaspoon cream of tartar

24 small Cream Puffs (page 35) filled with Crème Pâtissière Vanillée (page 45)

To make the caramel syrup: Place the sugar, water, and cream of tartar in a small skillet and stir over medium heat until the sugar dissolves. Bring the mixture to a boil and let cook, swirling the pan, until it turns a dark golden brown; this will take about 15 minutes. A knife dipped in the mixture should pull forth a soft thread; a candy thermometer will register 230°–234°F.

To make the croquembouche: Dip the bottoms of the cream puffs, one by one, in the hot caramel. Working quickly, stack them one atop another, forming a pyramid about 5 rows high.

Dip a fork into the remaining caramel, and wave the fork over the pyramid. Repeat until the whole is laced with golden threads.

Italian Bongo

This is a less spectacular but easier-to-serve dessert than Croquembouche (page 47), which it resembles.

Serves 8 to 12

One 8-ounce package semisweet
   chocolate chips
¼ cup milk
Crème Chantilly (page 43) made from
   1 cup of heavy cream, 1 tablespoon
   confectioners' sugar, and
   1 teaspoon vanilla

24 small Cream Puffs (page 35) filled
   with Crème Pâtissière Vanillée
   (page 45)

Melt the chocolate chips and milk together until the chips dissolve. Cool.
Pile the Crème Chantilly in the center of a round serving dish. Arrange the cream puffs around and on top of it in a mound. Pour the cooled chocolate syrup over all. Chill for at least 2 hours before serving.

Kaiserschmarren or Emperor's Dessert

Traditionally, this pancake is served by tearing it into pieces. I don't know a better way to serve it.

Serves 6 to 8

½ cup butter, at room temperature
1 teaspoon vanilla
½ cup granulated sugar
⅛ teaspoon salt
Zest of ½ lemon
6 egg yolks

1⅓ cups all-purpose flour, stirred, scooped, and leveled
1 cup milk
4 egg whites
½ cup raisins (optional)
Vanilla-Sugar (page 141)

Preheat the oven to 350°F. Butter a shallow baking pan.

Cream the butter and vanilla, then add the sugar, salt, and lemon zest and beat until fluffy. Add the egg yolks one at a time, beating after each addition. Add the flour and milk alternately, a large spoonful at a time, beating after each addition.

Beat the egg whites until stiff and fold into the batter together with the raisins, if desired. Pour the mixture into the baking pan and bake for about 40 minutes or until golden brown. While still hot, tear into serving pieces with 2 forks, held back to back, and sprinkle with Vanilla-Sugar. Serve with stewed fruit or a fruit puree.

TIP   *To tell when the egg whites are beaten stiff, tilt the bowl; whites should cling to the sides and not slide down.*

Lady Baltimore Cake

This cake has been popular for centuries. It took its name not from Lady Baltimore of the Calvert family, but for all the ladies in Baltimore, in whose honor it would be served. At the turn of the century, its popularity was given a boost by the author Owen Wister. It was served to him at the Women's Exchange in Charleston, and he was so impressed that he named a romance novel after the cake.

Serves 8 to 10

½ cup butter, at room temperature

1½ cups granulated sugar

2 large eggs, separated

2 cups cake flour, stirred, scooped, and leveled

1 teaspoon baking powder

½ teaspoon salt

1 cup milk

1 teaspoon vanilla

⅛ teaspoon cream of tartar

Preheat the oven to 375°F. Grease and flour three 8-inch layer pans; put a wax paper liner on the bottom of each.

Cream the butter and sugar. Add the egg yolks one at a time and beat well after each addition. Stir the flour, baking powder, and salt together. Alternate adding the dry ingredients, the milk, and the vanilla to the butter mixture, mixing after each addition. Beat the egg whites. When they are frothy, add the cream of tartar and continue beating until they hold soft peaks. Fold the whites into the cake batter.

Divide the batter among the cake pans, filling them half full. Bake for 25 minutes or until light brown on top and a cake tester comes out clean.

Let the layers cool for 10 minutes before turning out onto a rack. Let cool *completely*. Fill with Lady Baltimore Cake Filling (page 178) and frost with Summer Buttercream Frosting (page 182).

TIP   *When folding in egg whites, stir one-third of the whites into the batter first to lighten; then fold in balance of the whites.*

Lazy Man's Crème Pâtissière

If you can make gravy, you can make this!

Makes 2 cups

1 cup milk
4 tablespoons all-purpose flour
3 egg yolks, beaten lightly
1 cup butter or margarine, at room
   temperature

2 cups confectioners' sugar
2 teaspoons vanilla

In a small saucepan, slowly blend the milk into the flour until it makes a paste. Stirring constantly, cook over medium heat until the mixture thickens and becomes hard to stir. Remove from the heat and immediately stir into the beaten egg yolks. Let the mixture cool to lukewarm. Cream the butter with the confectioners' sugar; add the vanilla. Stir in the egg mixture and beat until well blended. Chill.

Meringue, Italian-Style

This meringue is a favorite with professional cooks because it doesn't bead or weep, and it keeps longer. It's a bit messy to make but worth the bother. This is the preferred coating for Baked Alaska (page 104).

Makes 3 to 4 cups

1 cup granulated sugar
⅓ cup cold water
4 large egg whites, at room
 temperature

¼ teaspoon cream of tartar
1 teaspoon vanilla

In a 1½-quart saucepan, combine the sugar and water. Cook over medium heat, stirring occasionally, until the sugar is completely dissolved (you won't hear a scratchy sound when you stir it). Increase the heat and bring the mixture to a boil; cook uncovered and without stirring until the mixture reaches 234°–238°F. on a candy thermometer or forms a soft ball when dropped into ice-cold water.

In the meantime, in the large bowl of an electric mixer, beat the whites on medium to high speed until foamy. Add the cream of tartar and vanilla and continue to beat until the whites hold soft peaks.

(cont.)

Once the syrup reaches the right temperature, while still beating at medium speed, slowly pour the syrup into the whites. It will splatter like crazy. Don't worry; don't scrape, and just keep pouring. Continue beating until the whites are glossy and the peaks stand straight up when you raise the beaters. Use in Spoom (page 87) or in place of the uncooked meringue in the Spanische Windtortes (page 82).

Napoleons

This layered puff pastry and cream-filled temptation is not half as difficult to make as you would think.

Makes 6 to 8 Napoleons

1 recipe Puff Pastry (page 64), or
   1 (17¼ ounce) package frozen puff
   pastry sheets, thawed
1 recipe Crème Pâtissière Vanillée
   (page 45)

1 recipe White Fondant Icing
   (page 184)
1 (1 ounce) square semisweet
   chocolate, melted

Line a cookie sheet with parchment paper if you have it, otherwise use as is.

On your work surface, roll out the Puff Pastry to almost the same size as the cookie sheet. (Remember, it puffs upward, not outward.) Cut the pastry in half crosswise by rocking a knife back and forth through the dough. Transfer the Puff Pastry to the cookie sheet by draping over your rolling pin. Prick every half inch with a fork and chill for 30 minutes while you preheat the oven to 400°F. Bake the chilled dough for 10 to 15 minutes, until lightly puffed and golden brown. Let cool on the cookie sheet to room temperature.

Fill a large pastry bag fitted with a large plain tip with the Crème Pâtissière Vanillée. Pipe out the crème in rows ½ inch high and cover the surface of one half of the Puff Pastry. Cover with the other half of the pastry, pressing down gently but firmly until the filling just starts to ooze out the sides. Frost with the White Fondant Icing and decorate with the melted semisweet chocolate piped in straight parallel lines about 1 inch apart. To give it the traditional "Napoleon" effect, drag a knife toward you across and at right angles to the lines. Repeat every 2 inches. Turn the cake around and drag the knife through the opposite way between the pulled lines. Freeze until firm, trim the edges, and cut into individual pieces. Serve at room temperature.

TIPS *Thicker is not better with puff pastry. The thinner you roll it, the easier it is for the dough to puff up without getting out of control. Some bakers place a cake rack over the pastry before baking so the pastry can go so high and no higher.*

If you don't have a pastry bag, a sturdy food storage bag with a corner snipped off is an effective substitute.

Norwegian "Spare" Pudding

From my Scandinavian beginnings, a pudding-cake to serve with a very American vanilla sauce.

Serves 8

½ cup butter, melted
½ cup granulated sugar
½ cup maple syrup
2 large eggs, well beaten
½ cup all-purpose flour, stirred, scooped, and leveled

½ teaspoon salt
1 teaspoon baking soda
½ cup milk

Preheat the oven to 350°F. Grease a 4-by-8-by-2½-inch loaf pan.

In the large bowl of an electric mixer, combine the butter and sugar and beat until fluffy. Add the syrup and beat well. Add the eggs and beat until fluffy. Add the flour, salt, and soda and combine gently. Add the milk, mixing only until incorporated. Pour the batter into the loaf pan and bake for 20 minutes.

Serve warm with whipped cream or with Vanilla Sauce, Circa 1917 (page 68).

TIP *If you don't have maple syrup, substitute regular (not "lite") pancake syrup.*

Oeufs à la Carmen

This is an orange-flavored variation of the classic meringue dish. And a very colorful version it is, too, with its mountain of "snow" arising out of a sea of red. Despite its name, it is not a Spanish but a German version of the French dish.

Serves 6

12 Oeufs à la Neige (page 59)
2 envelopes unflavored gelatin
¼ cup orange juice
1 cup heavy cream
2 tablespoons confectioners' sugar
   (remove big lumps)

1 teaspoon vanilla
1½ teaspoons curaçao
1 cup raspberry puree, preferably
   fresh, sweetened to taste
¼ cup chopped pistachios

Prepare the snow eggs. Soak the gelatin in the orange juice in a microwaveproof container for 5 minutes or until most of the orange juice is absorbed. Melt the gelatin–orange juice mixture in the microwave on HIGH for 40 to 50 seconds and let stand until the gelatin is completely dissolved. Beat the heavy cream in a chilled small mixing bowl with cold beaters at high speed. When it will hold a stiff peak, reduce the speed and add the sugar and vanilla. Slowly dribble the gelatin into the whipped cream. Stir in the curaçao. Heap the cream in the center of a glass bowl, forming a dome. Chill in the refrigerator until set. When ready to serve, lean the snow eggs against the whipped cream, pour the raspberry puree around the eggs, and sprinkle with chopped pistachios.

TIP *If you use a glass or Pyrex measuring cup, you can measure and microwave the juice in the same container.*

Oeufs à la Neige

Americans call this Floating Island (literally, "snow eggs"). Also we put the poached meringues on top of the custard; the French nap the meringue puffs with the custard. The results are the same: ethereal. You can also serve the snow eggs on a raspberry puree or surrounded by fresh fruit. For a fancier dish, use Austrian Custard Sauce (page 32) instead.

Serves 6

4 eggs, separated	1½ cups milk
1 cup granulated sugar, divided	½ vanilla bean

With an electric mixer, beat the egg whites until stiff. Continue beating, adding ¾ cup of the sugar ¼ cup at a time, until the mixture is no longer gritty. (It still is? Beat some more.)

In a large frying pan, heat the milk and vanilla bean to just simmering. Using 2 spoons, dipped in hot milk, scoop up approximately 4 tablespoons of white, making each "egg," well, egg-shaped. Place gently on top of the milk. Do not crowd. After 2 minutes, turn over and let cook another 2 minutes or until the "eggs" have expanded and become firm. *Do not let the milk boil.* Remove each "egg" from the milk with a skimmer and drain on a wet tea towel. Repeat until all the whites are used.

(cont.)

To make the custard sauce: Combine the leftover milk, the egg yolks, and the remaining ¼ cup sugar in a 2-quart saucepan, and cook over medium heat, stirring constantly until thick. If you wish to be classically correct, strain the custard before allowing to cool.

Pile the snow eggs in one deep dish or individual dishes (you can use toasted Pound Cake [page 62] as a base) and coat with the sauce. Garnish with slivered almonds, dollops of sweetened whipped cream, or maraschino cherries. Serve with Vanilla Pretzels (page 145).

TIP *A wet tea towel is used to drain the "eggs" so they won't stick.*

Oeufs à la Religieuse

Once you've mastered the making of snow eggs, there's much you can do with them. Traditionally, they have been served with a custard sauce. The chocolate version takes its name from the image of the black and white coif of the nun.

Serves 6

12 Oeufs à la Neige (page 59)
1 cup reserved hot poaching milk
2 egg yolks
¼ cup superfine sugar
4 squares semisweet chocolate,
   coarsely chopped

1 teaspoon vanilla
¼ cup crushed praline or finely
   chopped almonds

Prepare the snow eggs as directed on page 59, reserving 1 cup of the poaching milk. Beat the egg yolks and sugar in a 1½-quart saucepan, then gradually add the hot poaching liquid. Add the chocolate and cook over medium heat, stirring frequently, until the mixture thickens and will coat a spoon. Add the vanilla. Strain the custard and chill. When ready to serve, place the "eggs" in a serving bowl and nap with the cold chocolate sauce, then sprinkle with the crushed praline or chopped almonds.

TIP *One way to tell if a custard is properly thickened is to draw a line with your finger down the back of the spoon. If the line is distinct and stays that way, the custard is done.*

Pound Cake

Why is it called pound cake? Simple. The name is derived from the ingredient list: a pound of butter, a pound of eggs, a pound of sugar, and a pound of flour. Sometimes the basic formula was amended to a pound and a pinch, the pinch being baking powder (and a mighty big pinch it would have had to be!). In Great Britain, pound cake usually refers to a fruited cake which contains—you guessed it—a pound of fruit. If you've never had a homemade pound cake, I suggest you try this one.

Makes 1 large cake or 2 loaf cakes

2 cups butter, at room temperature (1 pound butter)
2¼ cups granulated sugar (1 pound sugar)
Ten 2-ounce (extra-large) eggs (1 pound eggs)

4 cups all-purpose flour, stirred, scooped, and leveled (1 pound flour)
1 tablespoon vanilla (optional)
1 tablespoon baking powder (optional)

Preheat the oven to 350°F. Butter and lightly flour a 10-by-4-inch tube pan or two 9-by-5-by-3-inch loaf pans. Line the bottom with wax paper; butter and flour the liner.

In the large bowl of an electric mixer, cream the butter. Add the sugar

½ cup at a time, beating well after each addition. Continue beating until the mixture is fluffy. While still beating, add the eggs two at a time. With the mixer running on the lowest speed, fold in the flour (and optional baking powder) by adding it ½ cup at a time as fast as you can. Add the vanilla last and mix just until incorporated. (Overbeating makes the cake rubbery.)

Pour the batter into the pan. Hold the pan about 1 inch above the countertop and drop to remove any large air holes. Bake in the tube pan for 1½ hours, in loaf loaf pans for 1 hour, or until a cake tester comes out clean. Check the cake periodically after the first 45 minutes to see if it's getting too brown. If it is, cover lightly with a sheet of aluminum foil.

Cool the cake in the pan on a rack for 10 to 15 minutes. Turn out of the pan and remove the paper liner. Invert once again onto the rack to finish cooling. Be sure the cake is completely cool before slicing. Store at room temperature.

TIPS   *I save the wrappers from sticks of butter just for the purpose of lining pans.*

Cover your mixer with a tea towel while adding the flour so that you don't have a lightly floured kitchen as well.

Puff Pastry,
Quick and Classic

Making your own is not as quick as buying the stuff ready-made, but not as hard and time-consuming as you may have been led to believe. According to Auguste Escoffier, considered the father of grand cuisine, "to get a perfect puff pastry, the two ingredients which constitute it [the dough and the butter] must be of exactly the same consistency." To do so, bakers have always chilled the dough, then done handstands to make the butter right. Some recipes suggest kneading it under cold running water; others suggest whacking it with a rolling pin.

Don't worry. With this recipe, instead of starting with cold butter and trying to soften it, you'll start with room-temperature butter and let the refrigerator harden it. Yes, there's still a fair amount of rolling to do, but it doesn't take muscles and goes fast. (With the quick method, you don't even roll it, you fold it.) It still takes time, but for most of that time, the refrigerator is doing the work.

Makes one 12 x 18 inch sheet

2¼ cups all-purpose flour, stirred, scooped, and leveled
¾ cup cake flour, stirred, spooned, and leveled

1 to 1¼ cups cold water
1 pound butter, in quarter-pound sticks, at room temperature

Place the flour in the large bowl of an electric mixer (use a flat whip if you have one) or in a food processor fitted with a dough blade. With the mixer running on slow, gradually add 1 cup water, plus enough more to form a soft, stringy dough. If you're using a food processor, pulse until the dough forms a ball. Chill, covered, in the refrigerator for about 1 hour.

The quick way to work it: On a lightly floured board, roll the dough out to approximately 16 inches square. Divide the butter into quarters and set three-quarters aside. Working with the remaining butter, spread half over half of the square, using your fingers. Fold the unbuttered half over the buttered half. Spread half of the remaining butter over half of the rectangle formed. Fold the unbuttered half over the buttered half. Spread the remaining butter on half of this and fold the unbuttered half over the buttered half. Wrap the dough in plastic wrap and chill in the refrigerator for 1 hour.

Repeat rolling, buttering, folding, and chilling three more times. After resting the fourth time, the pastry is now ready to be worked. However, it will keep, plastic-wrapped, for several days in the refrigerator or it can be frozen. Keep chilled until ready to roll out. Then rechill for 30 minutes just before baking.

The classic way to work it (with a few modern revisions): On a lightly floured board, roll the dough into a rectangle about 12 by 18 inches. The long side should be parallel to you. Over the right-hand two-thirds of the dough, using your hands, spread one-third of the butter. Then, as if folding a business letter, fold the unbuttered third to your left over onto the buttered middle third. Now bring the right-hand third, also buttered, over onto the middle. The folds should now be perpendicular to you. Wrap in plastic wrap and chill in the refrigerator for 30 to 60 minutes. This is considered one "turn." (Chefs who have multiple packages of puff pastry chilling mark each one with indents to denote the number of turns done.)

Remove from the refrigerator and unwrap the dough. Roll across the folds into a 12-by-18-inch rectangle, but this time the short side should be closest to you. Fold as before, letter fashion, the top third over the middle third, the bottom third up over both portions. Now turn so the folds are again perpendicular to you. Roll it out still a third time and fold it again. Roll it out a fourth time and spread the room-temperature butter over two-thirds of it as you did before. Fold into thirds and chill for 50 to 60 minutes.

Repeat the entire process two more times, omitting the butter in last "turn."

The pastry is now ready to be worked but will keep, plastic-wrapped, for several days in the refrigerator or can be frozen. Keep chilled until ready to roll out. Roll out and rechill for 15 to 30 minutes just before baking.

TIP *You can make puff pastry using whipped butter. You'll use less butter and the butter is more workable.*

VARIATION

Palmiers *For the last two turns, instead of using flour on the board, use Vanilla-Sugar (page 141)—and lots of it. After the final chilling, preheat the oven to 425°F. Roll the pastry out on the board into a 14-inch square, about*

¼ inch thick. Cut the square in two crosswise. Bring the two ends of one rectangle to meet in the center, then bring one folded edge over to meet the other. Repeat with the other rectangle. Chill each for 15 minutes. Cut cross-wise into ⅜-inch slices. Turn cut side up and place in staggered rows on cookie sheets (remembering these should triple in size while baking). Bake for 8 to 10 minutes, until the leaves begin to brown on the bottom. *Turn upside down and bake for 3 to 4 minutes more. Let the cookies cool on a rack, but they mustn't touch or they will stick to each other.*

Rice Pudding with Vanilla Sauce, Circa 1917

While researching my first cookbook, I found this recipe in a cookbook by Janet Mackenzie Hill, the Julia Child of the turn of the century. I decided to try it—especially since this is the only vanilla sauce I've ever found made with water not milk! I was in for a pleasant surprise. The sauce is light, not terribly sweet, and very subtly vanilla flavored. Try it poured over Pound Cake (page 62) or, with the addition of ½ cup rum, on Savarin (page 71) or babas.

Serves 6

RICE PUDDING

3½ tablespoons long-grain rice   2 tablespoons granulated sugar
2 cups hot milk   ½ teaspoon salt (optional)

Bring the rice, milk, sugar, and salt just to a simmer over medium-high heat, stirring occasionally. Reduce the heat and simmer gently, uncovered, and stirring frequently, until the liquid is just barely absorbed and the rice is tender, about 1 hour. Serve in individual bowls. Top with the hot Vanilla Sauce.

TIP   *This is a good way to use plain leftover rice. Reheat 1½ cups rice for 10 to 15 minutes with ½ cup milk and 2 tablespoons granulated sugar.*

VANILLA SAUCE

2 teaspoons cornstarch   2 tablespoons butter
1 cup granulated sugar   1 to 2 teaspoons vanilla
1 cup boiling water

Put the cornstarch in a 1½-quart saucepan and mash to remove any large lumps. Add the sugar and boiling water. Bring to a boil, then reduce the heat to a simmer. Cook for 10 minutes. Add the butter and stir until melted.

Allow to cool for a few minutes, and then add the vanilla. Taste and add more vanilla if necessary. Best served warm. Makes 1 cup.

TIP   *If you're using the sauce over cake, use 2 teaspoons of vanilla.*

VARIATION
Rum Syrup   *Use 1 to 2 teaspoons Vanilla-Rum (page 133) in place of the vanilla.*

Rice Trautsmannsdorf

This is the Cadillac of rice puddings, worthy of your finest glass serving dish. The quantity given here will serve twelve, so you might want to halve the recipe.

Serves 12

One 4-inch piece of vanilla bean
6 cups milk
½ cup long-grain rice
½ teaspoon salt
Water to cover
Zest of 1 lemon, grated

2 tablespoons granulated sugar
  (or to taste)
4 cups whipping cream
One 10-ounce jar seedless raspberry
  preserves
1 to 2 tablespoons Chambord

In a 3-quart saucepan soak the vanilla bean in the milk for 20 minutes. Simmer the rice in salted water to cover for 10 minutes. Drain and add the rice to the milk. Simmer the mixture for 45 to 60 minutes or until the rice is soft. Add the grated lemon rind and sugar. Let the rice cool thoroughly. Remove the vanilla bean.

Whip the cream until stiff and fold into the rice mixture. Place in a serving bowl and chill until ready to serve.

Heat the raspberry preserves until melted. Add the Chambord. Cool. Pour some of the raspberry syrup over the pudding and serve the balance in a sauce dish or gravy boat.

TIP *Remember the dish will be served cool, which will dilute the sweetness, so make the rice on the sweet side. If you wish, you can serve the raspberry syrup warm, but then serve all of it separately.*

VARIATION

Raisin Rice *Add ½ cup seedless raisins (or more) when you add the lemon rind.*

Savarin

This sweet yeast dough is considered one of the three challenges of patisserie, along with Puff Pastry (page 64) and Angel Food Cake (page 118). Traditionally, it is whipped by hand for what seems like hours, but if you have an electric mixer, especially one with a flat whip, it's a snap. I use the traditional sponge-yeast method because it uses fewer big bowls and leaves the kitchen in better shape. I also think the finished cake has a finer crumb. However, if you wish, you can proof the yeast in the milk and then mix all the ingredients through the eggs before settling the dough to rise. Punch it down by flipping it once or twice, then proceed with the recipe.

Serves 8 to 10

½ cake compressed baker's yeast
⅓ cup warm not hot milk
1 cup all-purpose flour, stirred, scooped, and leveled
1 cup cake flour, stirred, spooned, and leveled

½ teaspoon salt
1 teaspoon vanilla
3 eggs
1 tablespoon granulated sugar
½ cup butter, at room temperature

Mash the yeast with the warm milk and dissolve. Add ½ cup of the all-purpose flour and mix until smooth. Place in a warm place until the sponge gets bubbly and falls, about 1½ hours.

(cont.)

In the large bowl of an electric mixer, place the yeast, the rest of the all-purpose flour, the cake flour, the salt, and the vanilla. Mix the ingredients at the lowest speed with the flat whip. Add the eggs one by one, then increase the speed to medium and mix until the dough becomes smooth and elastic; the dough will simultaneously cling to the sides of the bowl and stretch to meet the beaters. If you're using a flat whip, the dough should suddenly ball up. (A professional-strength mixer might take 5 minutes, a weaker one 20 to 30. If your mixer can't handle it, do it by hand—*literally*—not spoon or spatula—the heat from your hand speeds up the process.)

Soften the dough by adding the sugar, then the butter, 1 tablespoon at a time. The dough should stretch easily between your fingers.

Oil well a 4-cup ring mold, including the top edges, and set aside.

Turn the dough out onto a lightly floured board (it will be very soft) and shape into a long roll. Cut it in half and fit one-half at a time into the mold. Level the dough as best you can and place in a warm place to rise again.

Preheat the oven to 375°F. Bake the ring for about 25 minutes or until the top is nicely browned and a tap on top elicits a hollow sound.

Turn out and if serving the same day, immediately pour Rum Syrup (page 69) over it.

Serve with the center filled with Crème Chantilly (page 43), Crème Pâtissière Vanillée (page 45), stewed fruit, a fruit salad, or ice cream balls. Savarin will keep in the refrigerator for a week if unsoaked and well wrapped.

Use a glass measuring cup to make the initial sponge. You'll see where it has doubled in bulk and again that it has fallen. Use a skillet to hold the ring while pouring the sauce over it. It makes it easy to pour out the excess sauce.

Sometimes removing the savarin from the mold is easier said than done. If your savarin won't come out, wrap the whole thing while hot in aluminum foil and let sit for 15 minutes or longer. Or, run a knife around the edge. Turn the mold over to get at the center to break the seal and use a fork to gently pull the savarin out.

Schaum Torte

If you've ever had an angel pie, this is its European ancestor. I use my mother's recipe—I have been making it for thirty years and never had a disaster (knock on wood!). This recipe is the only one I've ever seen that calls for baking powder; it results in a fluffy, moist, chewy meringue.

Serves 8

4 egg whites	1 teaspoon vinegar
½ teaspoon baking powder	1 teaspoon vanilla, preferably Bourbon
⅛ teaspoon salt	
1 cup granulated sugar, sifted if lumpy	1 teaspoon water

The vinegar, vanilla, and water are combined.

Beat the egg whites with baking powder and salt, until stiff. Add the sugar by the tablespoon, alternating with a few drops of the combined vinegar-vanilla-water. Continue beating until the sugar is thoroughly dissolved. Heap into a heavily greased 9-inch springform pan. Gently smooth the meringue and shape it halfway up the sides, creating a thick shell. Place in a cold oven and bake at 275°F. for 1 hour or more, or until delicately browned. Let cool until the pan is touchable, then run a thin knife inside to release the sides.

When completely cool, remove the sides of the pan. Serve the torte on the springform base placed on a serving plate. Fill with fresh fruit or any flavor instant pudding (in our house, we use vanilla—naturally!). Then top with 1 cup heavy cream, whipped, sweetened, and vanilla'd.

TIP   *Test to see if the sugar is dissolved by rubbing a small amount of the mixture between two fingers. It should not feel gritty.*

Sicilian Cassata

The national dessert of Sicily is the *Cassata* or Cabinet Cake. Done the traditional way, it is very similar to a free-standing trifle: A pound cake is split into thin horizontal slices and layered with a liqueur-enriched filling. The cake is then gently squeezed together, chilled, and iced. The result is a marvelous blendship of flavors, but rich, rich, rich! This version is both simpler and more vanilla-y.

Serves 8 to 10

CASSATA

1 recipe Lady Baltimore Cake (page 50)

Preheat the oven to 375°F. Butter and flour two 5-by-9-by-3-inch loaf pans. Fill one a little better than half full with the cake batter. Put the remaining batter in the second loaf pan—there should be ½ inch of batter. Bake both pans 25 minutes. Take out the smaller of the two loaves and set it out on a rack to cool in the pan; this will be the "lid." Bake the other loaf an additional 10 minutes; it should be brown and firm around the edges, soft and runny in the center. Remove the pan to a rack to cool. Allow to sit for 5 minutes, then scoop out the uncooked center of the larger loaf, forming a "cabinet" or shell. Discard the uncooked batter. Finish cooling and turn out of the pan. *(cont.)*

ITALIAN RICOTTA FILLING

One 1-pound container ricotta
2 tablespoons heavy cream
¼ cup superfine sugar
3 tablespoons vanilla liqueur, Bailey's
   Irish Cream, or Vanilla-Rum
   (page 133)

3 tablespoons coarsely chopped
   candied orange peel
2 squares semisweet chocolate,
   coarsely chopped

Beat the ricotta with an electric mixer until smooth. While still beating, add the cream, sugar, and vanilla liqueur. Fold in the orange peel and chocolate.

ASSEMBLY

Fill the shell with the traditional Italian Ricotta Filling. Put on the "lid." Chill. Dust with confectioners' sugar just before serving or cover with One-Minute Buttercream Frosting (page 179), either vanilla or chocolate.

TIP *The cassata may also be filled with fresh fruit, pudding, or whipped cream with chopped chocolate chips and/or maraschino cherries.*

Soubrics de Semoule

These are first cousins to Crème Frite. Serve the French way as a small entrée for luncheon with apple, quince, or red currant jelly, as a side dish with pork, or as a hearty breakfast with syrup and bacon.

Serves 6

3 egg yolks
1 whole egg
2 cups milk
4 tablespoons butter
½ cup granulated sugar

¾ cup plus 2 tablespoons semolina
   (Quick Cream of Wheat)
2 teaspoons vanilla
Butter for frying

Combine the egg yolks and whole egg in the small bowl of an electric mixer and beat lightly. In a 3-quart saucepan, bring the milk, butter, and sugar to a boil over medium-high heat. Sprinkle the semolina over the milk-sugar mixture and stir in, continuing to stir until the mixture gets quite stiff. (If it gets lumpy, don't worry.)

Remove the pan from the heat, and with the mixer running, gradually spoon the cooked mixture into the eggs. Add the vanilla. Pour into a well-greased jelly roll pan. Cool and chill until ready to sauté. Cut the mixture into round, square, or diamond shapes and fry in butter on both sides. Drain and serve.

TIP *If you have a portable mixer, you can do the whole thing in your cooking pot, provided you first incorporate some of the hot mixture into the eggs to warm them up and prevent their scrambling when mixed with the hot mixture.*

Soufflé Pudding And Quick Chocolate Sauce

This has the airiness of a soufflé but the staying power of a pudding.

Serves 6

8 tablespoons butter
Granulated sugar
One 4-inch piece of vanilla bean or
    2 teaspoons vanilla

¾ cup milk
4 eggs, separated
6 tablespoons butter, at room
    temperature

¾ cup all-purpose flour, stirred,
   scooped, and leveled
½ cup granulated sugar

¼ teaspoon salt
Quick Chocolate Sauce (recipe
   below) (optional)

Preheat oven to 375°F. Use 2 tablespoons of the butter to grease a 1-quart soufflé dish and sprinkle the sides with graulated sugar. Tap out the excess.

In a small saucepan, let the vanilla bean sit in the milk for about 20 minutes. Bring the milk and vanilla bean to a simmer and keep warm. Beat the egg whites until they hold stiff peaks.

Cream the butter in another saucepan. Blend in the flour. Remove the vanilla bean from the milk and pour the milk into this paste. Mix until smooth and cook for a few minutes to remove any raw flour taste. Remove from heat and add the sugar, salt, and egg yolks. Continue stirring.

When the mixture reaches the consistency of a thick custard, fold in the egg whites. Fill the soufflé dish three-quarters full and bake in a pan of hot water for 30–35 minutes. During cooking, the pudding should rise 1 to 1½ inches above the top of the mold. You can either serve this directly from the dish or, after letting it stand for a few minutes, turn it out of the mold onto a round dish. Serve with any vanilla-flavored custard cream, kirsch-flavored apricot jam, or Quick Chocolate Sauce.

(*cont.*)

TIP   Cover the top of the pudding with oiled wax paper when the top has become sufficiently colored.

QUICK CHOCOLATE SAUCE

8 ounces (1 cup) semisweet or milk chocolate chips

1 cup condensed milk or heavy cream

Melt the chocolate chips over hot water in a double boiler. Slowly blend in the condensed milk or cream and continue cooking until the mixture thickens.

TIP   Microwave! Melt the chocolate chips in a microwaveproof dish for 1 minute on HIGH. Stir, microwave another 30 seconds, and stir again. If necessary, repeat for another 30 seconds or until all the chips have melted. Slowly, blend in the condensed milk and microwave for another 30 seconds. The mixture will thicken while standing.

Soufflé Pudding de la Fleur de Marie

Also known as a Soufflé de Semoule, this is surprisingly light, naturally sweet, and a foolproof cold soufflé made with semolina.

Serves 6 to 8

3 eggs, separated
¾ cup granulated sugar, divided
2 cups milk

½ cup semolina (Quick Cream of Wheat)
1 teaspoon vanilla

Grease a 6-cup (1½-quart) soufflé dish or mold.

Beat the egg whites until very thick but not stiff. Very gradually add ¼ cup of the sugar, beating until stiff but not dry. Set aside.

Beat the egg yolks lightly in the small bowl of an electric mixer. Bring the milk and the rest of the sugar to a boil in a 3-quart saucepan over medium-high heat. Sprinkle the semolina on the milk, stirring to avoid lumps. Continue cooking and stirring until the mixture gets quite stiff. With the mixer running, gradually spoon it into the egg yolks. Mix until combined. Add the vanilla. Let cool.

Fold the egg whites into the cooled semolina mixture and pour into the prepared dish. Chill for about 4 hours.

(*cont.*)

Serve in the soufflé dish or unmold onto a plate and serve surrounded by fruit or swimming in a warm Quick Chocolate Sauce (page 80).

TIP *Don't worry if the semolina gets lumpy while cooking, the lumps will be beaten out when the cereal is beaten into the egg yolks.*

VARIATIONS
Chocolate Soufflé *Add 3 tablespoons cocoa to the milk before heating it.*
Coffee Soufflé *Add 2 teaspoons instant coffee to the milk before heating it.*
Raisin Soufflé *Stir ¼ to ½ cup raisins that have been soaked in 2 tablespoons rum into the mixture just before folding in the egg whites.*

Spanische Windtortes

This torte isn't Spanish at all but Viennese. Like Schaum Torte (page 73), this is a meringue-based confection. If you're out to have your friends oohing and aahing, make one large cake, but I think you'll get much more use out of these miniature versions. Best to do these the day before but not in a time of high humidity.

Makes 1 large or 6 small tortes

| 8 egg whites | 2½ cups superfine sugar |
| ½ teaspoon cream of tartar | 1 teaspoon vanilla |

Preheat the oven to 200°F. Very lightly grease and flour 3 large cookie sheets. On each sheet, invert a dish or cup about 3 inches in diameter and tap lightly to leave a faint guideline. Repeat until you have 18 circles. Don't let the edges touch.

In the large bowl of an electric mixer, beat the egg whites until foamy, then add the cream of tartar. When the whites begin to turn opaque, begin adding the sugar ¼ cup at a time, beating well after each addition. Add the vanilla. Continue beating until the whites are glossy and stand in stiff peaks. This may take as long as 10 to 15 minutes.

Put the meringue in a large pastry bag fitted with a plain tip. Make 6 bases by filling in 6 of the circles in a spiral, beginning at the edge and working toward the center. Use a wet spatula to smooth each.

With the rest of the circles, simply pipe a generous ring around the *inside* of the circumference of each. (You should have some meringue left over.)

Bake for 45 minutes; the meringues should be dry but not brown. You may have to bake in several batches. Remove from the oven and let the sheets cool before removing the meringues to a rack to cool completely. (If any break, don't despair—they're fixable.)

Using the leftover meringue, make 4 dots or gobs on the circumference of each base and, reserving the 6 best-looking rings for last, affix a ring to each. Return these pieces to the oven to bake for 20 minutes. Cool completely as directed above and repeat with the remaining circles. You should have 6 cases with walls 2 rings high.

If you wish, and have any meringue left over, even out the sides of the cases with additional meringue to create a smooth wall. Again bake for 20 minutes and cool.

Turn the oven off and return the cases to it to sit overnight.

The next day, fill the cases with fresh strawberries in any vanilla-flavored custard sauce, Crème Chantilly (page 43) mixed with halved maraschino cherries, or even a lemon filling (see Edna Edwards's Upside-Down Lemon Meringue Pie, page 97).

VARIATION
To make 1 spectacular torte, use an 8-inch cake pan to outline 4 circles. Fill in one completely to use as a base. Make a 1-inch-thick border around the inside circumference of each of two others. Form a lattice pattern in the fourth which will then become the top of the torte.

TIP   *If you don't have a pastry bag, use a triangle of waxed paper, rolled into a cone and stapled at top. Snip the point with a scissors. Use as is or fit it with a pastry tip.*

Spanish Vanilla Torte

A vanilla recipe with marzipan, almonds, and a chocolate layer? Yes, because of what the vanilla does to the other flavors: The whole is definitely more than the sum of its parts. Because of the marzipan, it will have the texture and chewiness of a brownie . . . and the chocolate makes it look and taste like one big chocolate chip cookie.

Serves 16

8 tablespoons butter

¾ cup almonds, flaked or coarsely ground

1½ (7-ounce) packages plain marzipan

½ cup superfine sugar

1 whole egg

3 egg yolks

1 tablespoon vanilla

⅔ cup all-purpose flour, stirred, scooped, and leveled

½ cup cornstarch, stirred, scooped, and leveled

5 egg whites

¼ cup sugar

2 squares semisweet chocolate, coarsely chopped

Apricot preserves, melted (optional)

8 ounces coating chocolate, melted, or one 8-ounce package semisweet chocolate, melted with 1 tablespoon shortening (optional)

Preheat the oven to 350°F. Use 2 tablespoons of the butter to grease a 10-inch springform pan. Sprinkle the sides of the pan with the flaked or ground almonds.

Melt the rest of the butter.

In the large bowl of an electric mixer, break up the marzipan into small pieces. Add ½ cup of the sugar, the whole egg, and the egg yolks. Beat until light colored and frothy. Add the vanilla. Blend in the flour, cornstarch, and hot butter. Beat until well combined.

In a clean bowl with clean beaters, beat the egg whites until frothy, then gradually beat in the rest of the sugar. Continue beating until the whites hold a stiff peak.

Fold the egg whites into the batter. Pour half of this mixture into the prepared pan. Scatter the coarsely chopped chocolate on top of this layer, then add the balance of the batter. Smooth off and bake for 40 to 45 minutes or until the cake has risen and then fallen.

Release the sides of the pan and immediately turn out the torte, placing it upside down on a rack to cool. (The bottom will become the top.) This can be served with just a dusting of confectioners' sugar, or to be very fancy, spread the top with apricot puree and then cover with the optional chocolate glaze. You can also puddle the glaze on top and let it ooze down the sides.

TIP *When adding the second layer of batter, spoon it into place. If poured, it forces the chocolate bottom layer to rise up around the sides.*

Spoom

This luscious dessert is all air and flavor. Although I suggest orange sherbet, you can use whatever flavor you like. The meringue, like any proper vanilla dish, will go with anything. Traditionally, this is served in champagne coupes, but use whatever you have.

Serves 12 generously

1 recipe Meringue, Italian-Style
   (page 53), chilled

½ gallon orange or raspberry
   sherbet, softened slightly

This can be made two ways: (1) Fold the meringue into the sherbet, letting streaks of meringue show. (2) Let the meringue cool in its bowl. Add the softened sherbet gradually to the meringue, blending at medium speed. Serve immediately.

VARIATION
Add a complementary liqueur (1 to 2 tablespoons per recipe) to the meringue after it has been beaten. Try Cointreau with orange spoom, or Chambord with raspberry.

Vanilla Soufflé

Of all the classic desserts, this is the most temperamental: Other foods wait for guests, but guests wait on the soufflé. However, to bring one to the dining room table to a chorus of oohs and aahs can be a marvelous experience.

Serves 8

One 4-inch piece of vanilla bean
¾ cup milk
3 tablespoons butter
⅓ cup all-purpose flour, stirred, scooped, and leveled

½ cup granulated sugar
4 egg yolks, beaten lightly
5 egg whites, beaten stiffly

Preheat the oven to 375°F. In a small saucepan let the vanilla bean sit in the milk for about 20 minutes, then scald the milk and bean and keep warm.

In another small saucepan, melt the butter and mix in the flour thoroughly. Immediately pour in the milk, whisking vigorously. Add the sugar and stir briskly over high heat until the mixture comes to a boil. Remove from the heat, and let cool slightly. Add a small amount of the mixture to the egg yolks and stir thoroughly, then pour the balance in. Beat well.

Stir about one-third of the beaten egg whites into the mixture to lighten it, then fold in the rest. Pour into a 6-cup soufflé dish (it should fill it three-quarters full). With your thumb, make a deep impression around the circumference of the soufflé, piling what you take out into the center. Bake for 25 to 30 minutes or until the soufflé has risen and turned a golden brown.

Serve immediately. To serve, hold 2 forks or serving spoons back to back and pull the crust apart. Dig deep into the soufflé for each portion, as the center should be quite saucelike.

TIP   *If you want your soufflé to stay puffed, at least for a time, start baking it in a water bath, but it must be baked for 5 to 8 minutes out of water before it is served. Another secret: Add 1 teaspoon baking powder to the flour.*

Enhancers

Vanilla is the ultimate complement to other flavors. Even if you can't taste it, you'll know if it's missing, as the folks at Coca-Cola found out.

According to *The Wall Street Journal*, for decades almost one-third of the world's vanilla crop was snapped up each year by the Coca-Cola Company. When the company took Coke off the market in 1985 and introduced the new Coke, world sales of vanilla plummeted. When Coca-Cola was forced to bring back the old Coke, rechristened Coca-Cola Classic, vanilla sales went back up to their previous levels. It doesn't take a genius to realize that the secret ingredient (or at least one of them) in the Classic recipe was vanilla.

Amber Tapioca Pudding

For those who think most tapioca puddings are a little on the bland side, this one has some kick. It's also a lovely coffee color thanks to the brown sugar.

Serves 4

¼ cup minute tapioca
1 cup firmly packed light brown sugar
2 cups cold water

Pinch of salt
1 teaspoon vanilla

Measure all the ingredients except the vanilla into a large saucepan and let sit for 5 minutes. Bring the mixture to a full rolling boil over medium heat, stirring constantly. (This will take anywhere from 5 to 10 minutes depending on how diligent you are in your stirring.) Cool and add the vanilla. The mixture will thicken more on cooling. Pour into individual serving dishes or a 1-quart dish. Serve immediately or chilled with Crème Chantilly (page 43).

Apple Breakfast Cake

The fragrance of this cake is guaranteed to awaken the most determined sleepyhead and perfume the whole house. Of course, if this is just a little too ambitious for you first thing in the morning, make it the night before. Besides being a great breakfast cake, it can be served for dessert as well. Top it with a caramel icing, serve floating in a sea of Crème Anglaise (page 40), or pour hot Vanilla Sauce, Circa 1917 (page 68), over it right from the oven.

Makes 12 large servings

¾ cup mild vegetable oil
1 cup granulated sugar
2 large eggs
2 teaspoons vanilla
1 teaspoon salt
1 teaspoon baking soda
2 teaspoons baking powder

2½ cups all-purpose flour, stirred, scooped, and leveled
1 cup coarsely chopped pecans
2½ to 3 cups peeled and coarsely chopped raw apples (I use Granny Smiths)

Preheat the oven to 350°F. Grease the bottom of a 9-by-12-by-2-inch baking pan and line with wax paper.

In a large mixing bowl, cream the oil, sugar, and eggs on low speed. Add the vanilla, salt, baking soda, and baking powder and blend well. Add the flour ¼ cup at a time, beating well after each addition. The batter will become very stiff and may be too hard to work for a lightweight mixer. In this case, blend the balance of the flour in by hand. Fold in the pecans and chopped apples. Then turn into the cake pan, spreading carefully; you will need to hold the wax paper in place as you do. Bake for 50 to 55 minutes or until brown on top and a tester comes out clean. Turn the cake out onto a cookie sheet, remove the wax paper, and then turn onto a cake rack to cool. The cake can be frozen but will keep for days if wrapped in aluminum foil.

TIP *If you are using a glass baking dish, reduce the oven temperature 25 degrees.*

Baked Cereal Pudding

Need an excuse to indulge in a light dessert? Consider this simply a different and delicious way to get your fiber.

Serves 6

4 cups milk	¼ cup granulated sugar
1 cup Grape-Nuts cereal	⅛ teaspoon salt
2 eggs, separated	1 teaspoon vanilla

Preheat the oven to 325°F. Lightly butter a 2-quart baking dish.

In a 3-quart saucepan, slowly bring the milk and cereal to a boil. (Stir occasionally; the Grape-Nuts will sink to the bottom where they might burn.) Remove from the heat. Cool until the bottom of the pan is comfortable to the touch; the mixture will thicken. Add the 2 egg yolks mixed with the sugar, salt, and vanilla. Beat the egg whites until stiff but not dry and fold in. Turn into the baking dish. Bake for 45 to 55 minutes or until the pudding is lightly browned on top. This pudding may be served hot or cold with light cream, Crème Chantilly (page 43), Crème Anglaise (page 40), or ice cream.

Chocolate Waffles

Invite some friends for dessert and serve these chocolate waffles with White Chocolate Butter (page 152) and some fresh strawberries. They're guaranteed to please.

Makes 4 to 5 waffles

½ cup butter, at room temperature
¾ cup granulated sugar
1 teaspoon vanilla
2 eggs, beaten
1¼ cups cake flour, stirred, scooped, and leveled

1 teaspoon baking powder
6 tablespoons cocoa
½ teaspoon salt (optional)

Cream the butter, sugar, and vanilla until light and fluffy. Add the beaten eggs and dry ingredients and stir until comparatively lump-free. Follow the directions for your waffle iron, but don't overcook or the chocolate will burn.

TIP *To keep the waffles crisp and warm while making the next batch, place in a brown bag and close tightly. Or put in a warm oven.*

Coca-Cola Cake

The proof of vanilla's empathy for Coca-Cola can be found in this recipe given to me by a friend from the South. When served at a dessert buffet, it looked, to be honest, like the ugly duckling of desserts. But those determined to sample everything exclaimed so over it, that long before the evening was gone, so was the cake.

Serves 18

2 cups granulated sugar
2 cups all-purpose flour, stirred, scooped, and leveled
1 teaspoon baking soda
1 cup butter

3 tablespoons cocoa
1 cup Coca-Cola Classic
½ cup buttermilk
2 eggs, well beaten
2 teaspoons vanilla

Preheat the oven to 350°F. Grease and flour a 13-by-9-inch pan.

Put the sugar, flour, and baking soda in a large mixing bowl and blend together. Bring the butter, cocoa, and Coke to a boil in a large saucepan, stirring constantly. Gradually pour over the dry mixture and mix well. Mix the buttermilk, eggs, and vanilla and add to the bowl, blending well. Pour into the pan and bake for 35 to 40 minutes or until a cake tester comes out clean. While the cake is still warm, pour hot Coke Icing over it.

(*cont.*)

TIP *Before measuring the buttermilk, rinse the cup with cold water. You'll find the buttermilk comes out easier.*

COKE ICING

½ cup butter
3 tablespoons cocoa
⅓ cup Coca-Cola Classic
3¾ cups Vanilla-Sugar (page 141) or
   1 (1-pound) box plain
   confectioners' sugar plus 2
   teaspoons vanilla

1 cup broken pecans (optional)
1½ cups mini-marshmallows
   (optional)

Bring the butter, cocoa, and Coke to a boil in a 3-quart saucepan, stirring constantly. Remove from the heat. Add the Vanilla-Sugar and stir until dissolved, then add the vanilla, if necessary. Pour over the cake while the cake is warm and the icing hot. Sprinkle pecans and/or mini-marshmallows over the top, if desired.

Edna Edwards's Upside-Down Lemon Meringue Pie

This is the pie that made my mother's dessert reputation. It came to be so popular that any time she brought it to a gathering of new friends, she brought copies of the recipe. (The vanilla cuts the acid in the lemon.)

Serves 8 to 10

1 recipe Schaum Torte (page 73)
4 egg yolks
Juice and zest of 1 lemon
½ cup granulated sugar
¼ cup water

¼ teaspoon vanilla
1 cup heavy cream, whipped
2 teaspoons confectioners' sugar plus
    ½ teaspoon vanilla (optional)

Make the Schaum Torte in a greased 9- or 10-inch pie plate, using a spoon to press into shape. Cook just 1 hour.

In the top of a double boiler or medium-size saucepan, beat the egg yolks until thick. Add the lemon juice and zest, the sugar, and the water and cook over medium-high heat until thickened. Cool, add the vanilla, then fold in half of the whipped cream. Fill the meringue shell. To the remaining cream, add the vanilla-flavored confectioners' sugar, if desired, and pipe rosettes or spread, like a meringue, over the top.

TIP *If you want to be really impressive (and the dessert decadently rich), use 1½ cups heavy cream, ½ cup for the filling and 1 cup on top.*

Eggnog Mousse

This could be done in a charlotte mold if you'd like, but my method is just as attractive, while being much easier to serve.

Serves 8

1½ envelopes unflavored gelatin	¼ cup whiskey
½ cup cold milk	1 teaspoon vanilla
3 eggs, separated	1 cup heavy cream, stiffly whipped
½ cup granulated sugar	1 package (12 double) ladyfingers

Lavishly butter a 9-by-4-by-3-inch loaf pan. (If you use a 5-inch-deep pan, you can line the sides with ladyfingers, separated lengthwise. Place the rounded side outward. In this case, you will need an extra package of ladyfingers.) In the top of a double boiler, soften the gelatin in the cold milk and dissolve over hot water. Beat the egg yolks until light, thick, and lemon colored. Add the sugar to the yolks and beat until thoroughly dissolved. Add the whiskey and vanilla and mix well, then add the gelatin/milk. Mix well. Fold in the cream. Beat the egg whites until stiff but not dry and fold into the mixture. Pour into the pan and chill in the refrigerator. When it begins to set (about 30 minutes), take a layer of ladyfingers, separated lengthwise, and press, rounded side down, crosswise across the top of the mousse. Finish chilling at least 3 hours. To serve, unmold and serve ladyfinger side down. Decorate with cherries or chocolate curls.

TIP   *To melt the gelatin in the microwave, measure the milk in a microwave-proof measuring cup. Sprinkle the gelatin over the milk and let sit for several minutes until the milk is absorbed. Microwave on HIGH for 40 seconds. Stir thoroughly and let sit to fully dissolve. Be sure to scrape all the gelatin out of the cup when you add it to the recipe.*

VARIATION

Eggnog Charlotte   *Separate the ladyfingers. Put enough aside to line the sides of a greased 1-quart charlotte mold or soufflé dish. Cut the rest into pie-shaped wedges and fit in the bottom of the mold. Place the reserved ladyfingers, rounded sides toward the outside, around the sides of the mold; they may extend above the top. Fill the mold with the mousse and chill. Before serving, trim the edges of the ladyfingers even with the top of the mousse. Turn out onto a plate and serve.*

Vanilla Ice Cream

According to the Ice Cream Council, 40 percent of all ice cream sold is vanilla. (The same goes for frozen yogurt and ice milk.) Not only that, another 50 percent of all ice cream choices *contain* vanilla. (The remaining 10 percent is chocolate except for a mere 1 percent which includes all the other single-note flavors.)

Unfortunately, the quality of vanilla ice cream varies from type to type and brand to brand. I prefer to make my own. As I said earlier, I collect ice cream makers as other people collect fine china.

In this section, I not only include homemade ice creams—my favorite vanilla ones—but dishes made with ice cream or made to be accompanied by ice cream.

Baked Alaska

When a chef wants to make a great splash, he trots out the Baked Alaskas. Actually, you can make one in your home with no great difficulty, providing you have a good freezer and an oven with a good broiler. The directions I give here are for the traditional rectangular shape, but there's no reason why you couldn't work with a round cake and a tall container of ice cream.

Serves 8 to 10

½ Pound Cake recipe (page 62),
    baked in a shallow 9-by-12-inch
    pan for 20 minutes or until done
¼ cup Vanilla-Rum (page 133)
    (optional)

½ rectangular gallon vanilla or
    Neapolitan ice cream, frozen *hard*
1 recipe Meringue, Italian-Style
    (page 53)

Preheat the oven to 450°F. Cut the Pound Cake 1 inch larger all around than the brick of ice cream. Place on a nonconductive surface—a bread or cutting board is fine—that has been covered with parchment paper trimmed to fit. Sprinkle with the Vanilla-Rum, if desired.

In the center of the cake, place the ice cream. Working quickly, spread the meringue with a spatula over the ice cream and cake; the meringue should be *at least* ½ inch thick. Make decorative swirls, but don't be so busy being fancy that the ice cream has a chance to soften.

Slide the board into the oven onto the second or third rack from the top; the meringue should not be immediately under the broiler unit. Let brown lightly for 3 or 4 minutes before checking. Don't open the door wide when you peek.

When browned, remove and serve immediately.

TIP   *The traditional garnish for a Baked Alaska is 4 egg shell halves, pushed into the meringue before it browns in the oven. When the meringue comes out, pour warm rum into the shells and ignite.*

Bombe

Bombes can be elaborate, involving many layers of different flavored ice creams and ices, or as simple as Neapolitan ice cream molded into a cylindrical shape. Typically, the bombe has two layers of ice cream and a center of whipped cream filled with goodies. (You could also use Real Vanilla Ice, page 112, in place of the whipped cream.) It's somewhat time-consuming, but the freezer does much of the work. This recipe is an adaptation of Sally Graham's ice cream cake.

Serves 8 to 10

1 quart chocolate ice cream
6 chocolate-covered toffee bars
   (I like Heath Bars)
1 pint coffee ice cream
1 cup heavy cream

2 tablespoons confectioners' sugar
1 teaspoon vanilla
Unsweetened cocoa
Quick Chocolate Sauce (page 80)
   (optional)

Chill an 8-cup ice cream mold or metal bowl in the freezer for at least 15 minutes. Remove the chocolate ice cream from the freezer and let soften.

Using a wooden spoon, pack the softened ice cream into the chilled mold to make a thick lining 1½ inches thick. Place in the freezer to harden for 30 minutes.

Chop the toffee bars coarsely and press two-thirds of them into the chocolate layer. Return the mold to the freezer for about 90 minutes or until firm. Remove the coffee ice cream from the freezer to soften for 15 minutes or so. Pack it into the mold, making an inner lining about 1 inch thick. Refreeze for at least 2 hours.

Beat the whipping cream in a chilled bowl with chilled beaters. Add the sugar and vanilla. Fold all but 1 teaspoon of the remaining chopped toffee bars into the cream and fill the center of the mold. Place plastic wrap against the ice cream and refreeze for at least 2 hours. (If you have any whipped cream left, you can make rosettes out of it by forcing through a pastry tube and then freezing on a cookie sheet.)

When ready to serve, chill the serving plate. Wrap a warm towel around the mold (or hold the mold in a bowl of hot water for a couple of seconds). Invert onto a plate, sprinkle with cocoa, and lightly dust with Vanilla-Sugar (page 141). Garnish with rosettes, if you've made them, maraschino cherries, or reserved toffee bars. Serve by slicing down through the bombe and cutting into wedges. Serve with Quick Chocolate Sauce, if desired.

TIP   *You can soften ice cream quickly in a microwave oven. Heat the ice cream on* MEDIUM-HIGH, *12 to 15 seconds, depending on the container size and shape.*

Corn Flake Ring with Ice Cream Balls

This is sheer heaven for my family: ice cream surrounded by candy. I don't serve it often, but there are days when nothing else will do.

Serves 6 to 8

1½ cups firmly packed soft brown or
    granulated sugar
1 tablespoon light corn syrup
½ cup milk

¼ cup butter
2 cups Corn Flakes
Vanilla ice cream

Mix the brown sugar with the corn syrup, milk, and butter and cook over medium heat until a ball forms in cold water (about 234°–238°F. on a candy thermometer). Butter a ring mold thoroughly. Place the Corn Flakes in a large mixing bowl, pour the hot syrup over, and mix gently. Pack lightly in a well-greased 6-cup ring mold. Cool at room temperature, covering with wax paper until ready to serve. Turn out onto a large platter. Place ice cream balls around and in the center of the ring. Serve with the Quick Chocolate Sauce (page 80) or fruit and whipped cream.

TIP   Don't *mix the hot syrup and Corn Flakes with your hands.*

Franco-Italian Ice Cream

Basic but not bland, light and luscious without being eggy or overpowering, it's a "French"-style ice cream because of the egg yolks, but made like an Italian meringue. This recipe makes 1 quart, and I could eat every bite of it myself.

Makes 1 quart

½ cup plus 2 tablespoons granulated sugar
⅛ teaspoon cream of tartar
6 tablespoons water

3 large egg yolks
1½ cups heavy cream
½ vanilla bean or 2 teaspoons vanilla

In a small saucepan, dissolve the sugar and cream of tartar in the water. Bring to a boil and boil without stirring for about 5 minutes or until the top of the syrup is covered with a froth of bubbles. A prewarmed candy thermometer should register 222°–228°F. Or, a spoonful of slightly cooled syrup, poured back into the syrup should form a long strand or thread. While the syrup is cooking, beat the egg yolks in the small bowl of an electric mixer until thick and light colored.

With the mixer on medium speed, slowly pour the hot syrup in a very fine stream into the egg yolks. When all the syrup has been incorporated, stop and scrape down the sides of the bowl. Increase the speed to high and beat until the mixture is very pale, and it and the bowl are cool. It can wait (do not stir) while you clean the beaters if necessary.

In a chilled bowl with chilled beaters (see Tips, page 43), whip the cream until soft peaks form. Slit the vanilla bean and scrape the seeds into the cream or add the extract. Fold the whipped cream into the yolk mixture.

Mellow the custard in the refrigerator for at least 2 hours, preferably overnight, before freezing. Follow the directions for your ice cream maker or use the "still-freeze" method.

Still-freeze method: Place the custard in ice cube trays without dividers. Freeze until ice crystals form around the edges; remove from the trays and beat until smooth. Refreeze and beat again when the mixture is almost solid. Freeze until solid.

Ice Cream Muffins

Nothing could be simpler or less work, but you would never know it from the results. These muffins are delicate and delicious, and I defy anyone to guess your secret. An excellent use for ice cream that has been stored too long and taken on a freezer taste. (If the off taste is pronounced, add 1 teaspoon vanilla to the batter.)

Makes 18 mini-muffins

1 cup single-flavor ice cream, softened (of course I recommend vanilla)

1 cup sifted self-rising flour

Preheat the oven to 350°F. Line mini-muffin tins with paper cups. Blend the ice cream and flour together until well mixed, but do not beat. Fill the muffin cups half full. Bake for 20 minutes, until the tops show some color. Serve warm or cold.

TIP   *Try serving these with White Chocolate Butter (page 152).*

Real Vanilla Ice

Not an ice cream, not a sherbet, not a sorbet, it's a real vanilla ice. A delightful dessert that's both low in fat and low in sugar, but high in taste appeal. It doesn't melt, it just softens, which makes it ideal for working with bombes and other molded desserts.

Makes 2¾ cups before freezing

3 cups skimmed milk
1 vanilla bean, split lengthwise
1½ envelopes unflavored gelatin
¼ cup cold water

2 tablespoons cornstarch
½ cup firmly packed light-brown
   sugar

Cook the milk and vanilla bean in a saucepan over medium-high heat, stirring occasionally, until bubbles form around the edge of the milk.

Sprinkle the gelatin over the water in a heatproof bowl and let sit until the gelatin swells and softens, about 2 minutes. In another heatproof bowl, mix the cornstarch and brown sugar.

When the milk is hot, pour approximately ¼ cup into the gelatin mixture and stir to dissolve. Add enough to the cornstarch-sugar mixture to form a thin paste. Pour the paste back into the pan of hot milk and heat, over medium heat, stirring constantly until thickened and bubbly. Turn the heat down and simmer for 5 minutes. Stir in the gelatin mixture. Cool to room temperature and then freeze according to the directions for your ice cream maker or still-freeze (see page 110). Before freezing, remove the bean pod.

VARIATION

For a white vanilla ice, replace the brown sugar with superfine granulated white sugar, decrease the cornstarch to 1 tablespoon, and add 1½ teaspoons Tahitian vanilla. This is the version to use as the center of your Bombes (page 105).

Rum-Vanilla Ice Cream with Chocolate-Cinnamon Sauce

The combination of rum/vanilla/chocolate/cinnamon is spectacular.

Makes 1 quart ice cream and 1 cup sauce

½ vanilla bean, ground with
   1 tablespoon granulated sugar
2 cups milk
6 egg yolks

⅞ cup granulated sugar
6 to 7 tablespoons Vanilla-Rum
   (page 133)
2 cups heavy cream

Soak the ground vanilla bean in the milk for 20 minutes. Slowly bring the milk to a boil in a heavy 3-quart saucepan over low heat. Strain. Beat the egg yolks and sugar in the large bowl of an electric mixer until they are thick and lemon colored and form a ribbon when the beaters are lifted. While still beating, slowly pour the hot milk into the yolk mixture. Return the mixture to the saucepan and stir over medium heat until the mixture thickens enough to coat the back of a spoon, 5 to 7 minutes. Add the Vanilla-Rum. Place the saucepan in a sink full of cold water to cool; stir occasionally to prevent a skin from forming.

In a chilled bowl, using chilled beaters, whip the cream until it stands in soft peaks. Fold thoroughly into the cooled egg mixture. Freeze according to your ice cream maker's instructions or still-freeze (see page 110).

CHOCOLATE-CINNAMON SAUCE

8 squares semisweet chocolate or one
   8-ounce package semisweet
   chocolate chips
¼ cup butter

½ cup light cream
1 teaspoon cinnamon (or to taste)
2 tablespoons Vanilla-Rum
   (page 133)

Melt the chocolate and butter in the top of a double boiler. Cook the light cream with the cinnamon in a small saucepan until bubbles form around the edge of the pan. Stir the chocolate mixture into the cream. Blend in the Vanilla-Rum. Taste; add more cinnamon if desired. Serve hot.

TIPS *Microwave instructions: Melt the chocolate and butter in a micro-wave-proof container on HIGH for 1 minute. Stir, cook for another 30 seconds, and stir again. Heat the cream and cinnamon in a glass measuring cup on HIGH for 45 seconds and repeat in 15-second increments until bubbly. Proceed with the recipe as above.*

This recipe can be doubled.

Vanilla Milk Shake

Ever try to make a milk shake at home in the blender? Mine were blah until I remembered the soda jerk always began by pouring some syrup into the shaker first. Eureka! I'd found the secret.

Makes 1 milk shake and 1 cup syrup

3 tablespoons Vanilla Syrup (recipe
  follows)
2 large scoops vanilla ice cream,
  slightly softened

¾ to 1 cup very cold milk

Put the ingredients, in the order above, in a blender and process until smooth and thick, adjusting the amount of milk for the thickness desired.

VANILLA SYRUP

1 vanilla bean, split
1 cup water

1 cup granulated sugar

Soak the vanilla bean in the water for half an hour. Pour the water, bean, and sugar into a heavy saucepan and cook over medium-high heat. Stir constantly until the sugar dissolves; bring to a boil. Boil for 5 minutes or until the mixture thickens slightly. Let cool to lukewarm. Pour through a strainer into an airtight container and store in the refrigerator. Keeps almost forever.

TIP *For a stronger vanilla flavor, leave the bean in place and only strain when you use.*

Javanilla

Javanilla? Never heard of that, you say? No wonder, it's my own coinage—Java plus vanilla—to describe one of the oldest and best flavor combinations in cooking: coffee and vanilla. And I felt I had to come up with a new one only because the right one, the correct one, the original one, for this coupling—mocha (which was the name of the seaport through which Arabian coffee was originally exported)—has been usurped by the chocophiles.

Did you know that it's the vanilla in coffee liqueurs such as Kahlua that makes them so smooth and full-bodied and distinctive? (Try doctoring cheap brands by sticking a vanilla bean in the bottle.)

The best proof of the perfection of this pairing? Take a tired vanilla bean that's been infused, rummied, or sugared. Grind it up and add a pinch to your coffee grounds. Heavenly.

Angel Food Cake

This is the only recipe for which I not only sift the flour but the sugar, too. Although surveys show that angel food cakes are the most popular of all cakes, many people consider them on the sweet side. The addition of a little coffee cuts the sweetness.

Serves 12

1½ cups sifted confectioners' sugar
1 cup sifted cake flour
10 large egg whites (1½ cups)
1½ teaspoons cream of tartar
1 teaspoon vanilla

1 tablespoon strong brewed black coffee (optional)
¼ teaspoon salt
1 cup granulated sugar

Preheat the oven to 350°F. Before measuring the confectioners' sugar and flour, sift each three times. Blend together.

Beat the egg whites until feathery. Add the cream of tartar, vanilla, coffee, if desired, and salt; beat until stiff but not dry. Continue beating as you add the granulated sugar, 2 tablespoons at a time. Beat well after each addition. If you've beaten the whites sufficiently, the sugar will have dissolved and the meringue will not be grainy to the touch. Gently fold in the flour mixture in quarters while rotating the bowl. Fold just until the flour disappears. Do not overmix.

Using large dollops, gently pile the batter into an ungreased 10-by-4-inch springform or tube pan with a removable bottom. Run a knife or spatula in concentric circles through the batter several times to remove any large air spaces. Bake for 50 to 60 minutes on the center rack or until the cake has turned brown, lost its moist look, and a tester comes out clean.

Do not remove the cake from the pan but immediately invert the pan onto a large funnel or soft-drink bottle. Let sit until cold—about 2 hours. Remove from the pan and frost with Fluffy White Icing (page 177), if desired.

TIP   *Use your three-screen flour sifter to sift the sugar first, then the flour. You will only have to put the ingredients through once. By sifting the flour last, you clean the sifter of sugar.*

Coffee Liqueurs

To be honest with you, I have as yet to find the perfect one. (My husband says that's because I enjoy the looking and the tasting too much to ever declare a winner.) I offer you three—each good and each different in its own way.

CARIBBEAN COFFEE LIQUEUR

Has a slightly molasses taste that is reminiscent of a Caribbean island.

Makes about 5 cups

1½ cups firmly packed brown sugar
1 cup granulated sugar
2 cups water
½ cup instant coffee

1 vanilla bean, split, or 2 tablespoons vanilla
3 cups vodka

Combine the sugars with the water in a 1½-quart saucepan. Bring to a boil and cook for 5 minutes. Gradually stir in the instant coffee. Cool. Pour into a 1-quart jar and add the vanilla bean and vodka. Shake well. Cover and let stand in a dark but cool place for at least 2 weeks before serving.

CUATRO LICOLES DE CAFÉ

More syrupy, with a stronger vanilla flavor. It must sit and brew for at least 4 weeks—the longer the better.

Makes ½ gallon

4 cups granulated sugar
4 cups water

½ cup instant coffee

2 vanilla beans   4 cups rum

Bring the sugar, the water, the coffee, and one of the vanilla beans (cut into 1-inch pieces) to a simmer in a large pot. Continue simmering for 45 minutes or more, until the mixture has thickened. Remove and let cool completely; add the rum and the second vanilla bean. Store in a dark bottle, if possible, in a cool, dark place for 4 weeks before using. Decant and strain into another bottle before serving.

CHERI'S KAHLUA

I find this not quite so strong as the other two, nor as sweet.

Yield ½ gallon

3 cups granulated sugar   A fifth of vodka
4 cups water   3 teaspoons vanilla
12 slightly rounded teaspoons of a
   good instant coffee (I use a
   gourmet one)

Bring the sugar, water, and coffee to a boil; lower the heat and simmer for 1 hour. Cool; add the vodka and vanilla. Pour into a clean bottle and let stand in a cool, dark place for 2 to 3 weeks before serving.

Coffee Whip

About as simple as a dessert can be . . . and an excellent example of the enhancing power of vanilla. Taste the dessert before and after you add the vanilla; note how the coffee flavor is strengthened yet smoothed out by the vanilla.

Serves 4

One 10-ounce package mini-marshmallows
9 ounces hot, strong coffee (If you're using instant, add 1½ teaspoons coffee to 9 ounces water)

1½ teaspoons vanilla
1 cup Crème Chantilly (page 43) or one 8-ounce container whipped topping, preferably made with cream

In a 3-quart saucepan over medium heat, dissolve the marshmallows in the coffee, stirring constantly. The mixture will get foamy and begin to thicken. Remove from the heat and let cool until the bottom of the pan is comfortable to the touch. Add the vanilla. Stir in 1 heaping tablespoon of the Crème Chantilly to lighten the mixture. Then fold in the rest; there should be light streaks in the mixture. Pour into an oiled 1-quart mold and chill. Unmold and serve in a pool of light cream or garnish with whipped topping.

TIP *Melt the marshmallows with the coffee in the microwave on* HIGH *for 2 minutes or until the marshmallows swell up. Stir. Repeat for another minute, then stir again. Repeat until the marshmallows are melted.*

French Nougat Candy

This may look like lots of trouble, but it isn't—your electric mixer does most of the work. The result of your efforts is a chewy, traditional, melt-in-your-mouth nougat that makes store-bought seem like rubber glue.

Makes 64 pieces

2¼ cups granulated sugar
1 cup light corn syrup
½ cup water
3 large egg whites, at room
    temperature
8 teaspoons of the lightest honey you
    can find

1 teaspoon instant coffee granules
1 teaspoon vanilla
3 tablespoons butter, at room
    temperature
¼ teaspoon salt
½ cup slivered almonds
Confectioners' sugar

Put the sugar, corn syrup, and water in a 2-quart saucepan. Cook, stirring frequently, over medium heat until the sugar is dissolved and the mixture loses its opacity. Continue cooking without stirring over medium-high heat until the mixture reaches the soft-crack stage (between 270° and 290°F. on a candy thermometer). Test by dropping a small amount from a wooden spoon into ice-cold water. It should separate into strands that can be stretched when removed from the water.

While the sugar is cooking, beat the egg whites in the largest bowl of an electric mixer until stiff.

In a small saucepan, heat the honey until boiling and add slowly to the whipped whites, beating continuously. Beat until the whites have doubled in bulk. Add the sugar syrup to the mixture in a slow, steady stream while beating on high. Do not scrape the saucepan to get the last drops. Continue beating until the mixture is very light but still chewy. It should still be hot.

Mix the coffee and vanilla with the butter and add to the mixture. It will deflate immediately. Add the salt and almonds. Taste. Add more coffee if the honey taste is too strong.

Oil or spray-grease an 8-by-8-inch pan. Line with oiled wax paper. Pour the mixture into the pan and when cool, store in the refrigerator. Turn out onto a confectioners' sugar–dusted board. Remove the wax paper and dust the nougat with more confectioners' sugar. Cut into 1-inch-square pieces and wrap individually, or store in a block in the refrigerator, cutting when needed.

Frozen White Russian

Like a White Russian, but better!

Serves 4

1 pint vanilla ice cream
2 ounces vodka

2 ounces Kahlua or Caribbean Coffee
Liqueur (page 120)

Mix all the ingredients in a blender or an electric mixer until smooth. Do not use a food processor. Pour into a plastic-wrap lined 5-by-3-inch pan, or into an ice cube tray without dividers. Put in the freezer and chill thoroughly. The dessert will not freeze through. Serve in scoops in champagne glasses, accompanied by a strawberry or two.

TIP *This recipe can be doubled and even quadrupled—it all depends on the capacity of your blender.*

Javanilla Pudding

What I like about this pudding-mousse is that its taste is only eclipsed by its ease of preparation. This is the type of dessert you can throw together at the last moment. Once you've melted the marshmallows, do all the rest in a metal bowl set inside a second bowl filled with ice cubes.

Serves 6 generously

½ cup strong brewed coffee, boiling, or 1 teaspoon instant coffee dissolved in ½ cup boiling water
2 dozen marshmallows, quartered, or 3 cups mini-marshmallows
1 teaspoon vanilla
1 cup heavy cream, whipped
¾ cup chopped pecans (optional)
Vanilla wafers or macaroons

Pour the hot coffee over the marshmallows and stir until the marshmallows have partially dissolved into small bits. Refrigerate until slightly jelled; the mixture should jiggle. Add the vanilla and beat until smooth. Fold in the whipped cream and nuts, if desired. Line a serving bowl or 9-by-5-inch loaf pan with vanilla wafers or macaroons. Pour in the coffee mixture. Chill in the refrigerator until set. Unmold and serve.

TIP *Before lining the bowl with wafers, line with plastic wrap. It makes removal so much easier.*

Marshmallows

I first made this recipe for my book *Oh, Fudge!* and it remains the best marshmallow recipe I've ever found. Interestingly enough, the coffee-vanilla combination results in a buttery taste. The recipe isn't difficult, but you should use a candy thermometer for the best results.

Makes 48 to 72 pieces

¼ cup cornstarch
¼ cup confectioners' sugar
2 envelopes unflavored gelatin
¾ cup cold brewed black coffee or
   1 teaspoon instant coffee dissolved
   in 2 tablespoons hot water plus
   enough cold water to measure
   ¾ cup

1½ cups granulated sugar
1 cup light corn syrup
¾ cup water
⅛ teaspoon salt
1½ teaspoons vanilla

For ½-inch-thick marshmallows, oil two 8-by-8-inch pans. Line with wax paper and lightly oil again. Mix the cornstarch and confectioners' sugar and sprinkle 1 heaping tablespoon of the mixture into the bottom of each pan. Reserve the remainder for later.

Mix the gelatin and cold coffee in a heatproof/microwaveproof measuring cup and let stand until the liquid is absorbed, 5 to 10 minutes. Dissolve the gelatin over hot water or in the microwave on high for 40 seconds. Place in the large bowl of an electric mixer.

Combine the granulated sugar, corn syrup, water, and salt in a heavy 2-quart saucepan. Stir constantly but not vigorously with a wooden spoon over low heat until the sugar dissolves. Increase the heat and bring to a boil. Wash down the sides of the pan with a pastry brush dipped in hot water to remove any undissolved sugar crystals.

Continue cooking without stirring over medium heat until the mixture thickens and clings to the spoon. Continue cooking until the syrup reaches the soft-crack stage (between 270° and 290°F. on a candy thermometer). Test by dropping a small amount from a wooden spoon into ice-cold water. It should separate into strands that can be stretched when removed from the water.

With an electric mixer on its lowest speed, slowly add the hot syrup to the gelatin. It will splatter at first, so watch out. When all of the mixture has been added, increase the speed slightly and beat until a froth covers the top; this will take 4 to 5 minutes.

Increase the mixer speed and add the vanilla. Beat at least 10 minutes or until the mixture becomes light, shiny, and fluffy and holds its shape on a spoon.

Spread the mixture in the sugared pans and refrigerate at least 4 hours.

Turn the marshmallows out onto wax paper covered with the balance of the cornstarch–confectioners' sugar mixture.

Cut with a sharp knife dipped in cold water. Roll the marshmallow edges in more of the mixture. Store in an airtight container in a cool place or in the refrigerator. The candy will be very soft for the first few days, then toughen up.

TIP *You can use a pizza cutter or cookie cutters, dipped in the cornstarch–confectioners' sugar mixture, to cut the candy.*

Mocha Cake

This is the one, the only, the original, mocha cake.

Serves 6 to 8

2 cups granulated sugar
½ cup water
8 egg yolks
2 cups unsalted butter, at room
   temperature

1 teaspoon vanilla
1 tablespoon brewed black coffee
One 12-ounce box vanilla wafers
1 cup strong brewed black coffee

Cook the sugar and water in a 2-quart saucepan. Bring to boil, stirring to dissolve the sugar. Let it simmer for about 10 minutes or until it thickens (about 230°F. on a candy thermometer) and a small amount tested in cold water drops to the bottom without dissipating. Remove from the heat and allow to cool for up to 10 minutes.

Be sure the egg yolks are free of the chalazae (the cords that keep the yolk centered), then beat until fluffy in a large mixing bowl and gradually pour in the hot syrup. Continue beating until the yolks have almost doubled in size and the mixture is cool.

Cream the butter in a large mixing bowl with the vanilla and 1 tablespoon black coffee. Beating at medium speed, add the egg-syrup mixture ¼ cup at a time. If the mixture shows any sign of separating, add no more syrup.

Grease a 1-quart loaf pan. Gently ease a large piece of plastic wrap down into the pan, pressing it against the sides and bottom of the pan. It should extend over the sides.

Quickly dip each vanilla wafer into the remaining strong black coffee and stand upright, rounded side out, around the sides of the pan. Then, put a layer of coffee-dipped wafers, rounded side up, on the bottom. Top with a thick layer of the buttercream and add a second layer of coffee-dipped wafers, then more buttercream. Add a second row of wafers around the sides; they will protrude above the pan, but don't worry about it. Continue alternating wafers and cream until the mold is full, ending with a layer of wafers. (You should have 4 layers of wafers and ½ to 1 cup of buttercream left over. Refrigerate it.) Cover the top of the pan with plastic wrap and refrigerate for several hours or overnight.

An hour or so before serving, remove the excess buttercream from the refrigerator and let come to room temperature.

With the assistance of the plastic wrap, turn the cake out of the loaf pan onto a serving dish. Decorate the top with the extra buttercream. Return the loaf to the refrigerator until ready to serve. Serve in very thin slices!

VARIATIONS

Vanilla Cake *Add 1 more teaspoon vanilla in place of the 1 tablespoon coffee.*

Coffee Cake *Substitute ½ cup strong black coffee for the water when making the sugar syrup. Reduce the vanilla to ½ teaspoon and do not use coffee when creaming the butter.*

Chocolate-Mocha Cake *Substitute ½ cup strong black coffee for the water when making the sugar syrup. Reduce the vanilla to ½ teaspoon but add 3 ounces of melted and cooled semisweet chocolate to the buttercream.*

TIPS *Break room-temperature eggs, one by one, into your hand. Let your hand act as a sieve, holding the egg yolk as the white falls through. Then snip each chalaza close to the yolk with a kitchen scissors. Just be sure not to be holding the yolk above your egg whites in case it should break.*

To eliminate air holes, top the completed loaf pan with a small weight—not too heavy or the buttercream will ooze around it. I use a 1-pound package (2 small tubs) of margarine.

Vanilla-Rum

That masterful food writer M.F.K. Fisher is on record as saying that anywhere you can use vanilla, rum is better. I can't agree. (You really wouldn't expect me to, would you?) For me, rum is too harsh, too overpowering. In fact, I prefer my rum vanilla'd.

I always add a vanilla bean to my cooking rum, and within two to three days, even a truly harsh bottle of rum will mellow. When the rum gets low, refill the bottle and continue doing so until you notice that the rum, after a week or so of contact with the bean, hasn't taken on a golden hue. Then it's time to retire the bean.

If you haven't had the chance to make some Vanilla-Rum beforehand, you can make a small amount the night before. Simply add a 2-inch piece of vanilla bean to ⅓ to ½ cup of rum, seal tightly, and allow to sit out overnight. Before using the rum, remove the vanilla bean, dry, and reuse.

However, to paraphrase Ms. Fisher, anywhere you can use rum, Vanilla-Rum is better.

Bread Pudding
with Rum Sauce

For those of you who think of bread pudding as old-fashioned or for children, this will convince you otherwise. It's as delectable (and easy) a dessert as you can serve.

Serves 6

3 tablespoons butter
¾ pound bread (try a French or
   Italian loaf), sliced
3 cups milk

1½ cups granulated sugar
2 extra-large or 3 medium eggs
1½ tablespoons vanilla
½ to 1 cup raisins (optional)

Preheat the oven to 350°F. Butter the bread on one side, break the slices into large chunks, and place in a large bowl. Pour the milk over it and stir once or twice to make sure all the bread is coated. With an electric mixer, beat the sugar, eggs, and vanilla until fluffy. Add to the bread mixture, combining well. Stir in the raisins, if desired.

Bake in a 7-by-12-inch pan until firm, about 90 minutes. If the top is browning too much, cover loosely with pieces of aluminum foil. Serve warm or cold, plain or with sauce.

To serve with Rum Sauce: Preheat the broiler. Cut the pudding at room temperature into slices or cubes. Place in a broilerproof au gratin pan or individual dishes. Spoon some of the sauce over the top, and run under the broiler until the top is golden brown and the pudding is heated through. Serve immediately with extra sauce on the side.

TIP *Instead of buttering the bread, put the butter in a 3-quart ovenproof casserole and place in the oven while preheating it.*

RUM SAUCE

½ cup butter	1 cup confectioners' sugar
1 egg, room temperature	2 to 4 tablespoons rum

Melt the butter; keep hot. Beat the egg in a small bowl until thick and lemon colored. Gradually add the sugar to the egg, beating until thick. Add the hot butter and stir—don't beat—until smooth. Blend in the rum to taste, enough to give it a pouring consistency.

TIP *You can substitute whiskey for the rum.*

Fruit with Rum

A simple, simply delicious dessert. Very refreshing on a summer's evening.

Serves 4

1 ripe cantaloupe or any other melon but watermelon	½ cup Vanilla-Rum (page 133)
1 quart strawberries, hulled	1 cup heavy cream
One 8-ounce can sliced pineapple in juice or light syrup, chunked	1 tablespoon confectioners' sugar (or more to taste)
	1 tablespoon vanilla

Cut the melon in half and slice off the rind. Cut the meat into chunks. Combine the fruits, toss gently with the Vanilla-Rum, and chill in the refrigerator.

Using chilled beaters and bowl, whip the cream. When it becomes frothy, add the sugar; when it holds stiff peaks, add the vanilla. Put the fruit mixture in individual dishes or on top of Pound Cake (page 62) slices. Top with the whipped cream and serve.

TIP   *If you want to be extra fancy, use a melon baller to cut up the melon.*

Rum Balls

A welcome change from the standard bourbon ball cookies served during the holidays, these Rum Balls are much more subtle and mellow, and hard for tasters to figure out the ingredients.

Makes 4 dozen

2 cups (approximately 50) finely ground vanilla wafers
1 cup finely ground pecans
1 cup confectioners' sugar
½ cup light corn syrup
¼ cup Vanilla-Rum (page 133) or ¼ cup rum plus ½ teaspoon vanilla
Confectioners' sugar

Combine the wafers and pecans. Mix with the confectioners' sugar, corn syrup, and Vanilla-Rum. Stir until all signs of the sugar disappear.

Roll the mixture into balls the size of walnuts, then roll in confectioners' sugar. Let stand for about 1 hour. If the balls have absorbed too much of the sugar, reroll them. Store in a cookie jar or tin. Will keep for several weeks if the family doesn't find them.

TIP *Coat your hands with confectioners' sugar before you roll the balls.*

VARIATION
Chocolate-Rum Balls *If you wish to make an entire chocolate batch, add*

2 tablespoons cocoa along with the confectioners' sugar. You can, however, satisfy both vanilla and chocolate lovers: Make 2 dozen vanilla balls, then add 1 tablespoon cocoa to the balance of the dough, and make 2 dozen chocolate.

Sally's Nesselrode Pie

Sally Duff was kind enough to share this recipe with me years ago; never have I made it when it didn't garner raves. What makes it extra special is that it makes *two* pies.

Makes two 10-inch pies

Two 10-inch pie crusts, baked until golden brown

CHOCOLATE LAYER

1 envelope unflavored gelatin
¼ cup cold water
½ cup boiling water
2 squares unsweetened chocolate, coarsely chopped

4 egg yolks, slightly beaten
1 cup granulated sugar
¼ teaspoon salt
1 teaspoon vanilla
4 egg whites

Sprinkle the gelatin over the cold water and let sit for 5 minutes or until the water is absorbed. In a large bowl, pour the boiling water over the chocolate and stir until smooth. Add the gelatin to the chocolate mixture and stir until dissolved, then add the egg yolks, ½ cup of the sugar, the salt, and the vanilla. Beat thoroughly. Cool in the refrigerator until the mixture begins to thicken. Beat the egg whites until foamy, add the remaining ½ cup sugar a little at a time, and continue beating until the whites are stiff. Fold into the gelatin mixture. Divide between the 2 pie shells and chill until ice cold and thick.

VANILLA LAYER

1 envelope unflavored gelatin
¼ cup cold water
3 eggs, separated
1½ cups milk
¾ cup granulated sugar
⅛ teaspoon salt
3 tablespoons Vanilla-Rum
   (page 133)

¼ cup each chopped red and green
   maraschino cherries
Crème Chantilly (page 43) or
   whipped cream (optional)
Sweet chocolate shavings (optional)

Sprinkle the gelatin on the cold water and let sit for 5 minutes or until the water is absorbed. In a large saucepan, beat the egg yolks; add the milk, sugar, and salt. Cook over medium heat, stirring constantly, until the mixture thickens and coats a spoon. Stir in the gelatin. Chill until the mixture begins to jell. Beat the egg whites until stiff and fold into the cooled custard along with the Vanilla-Rum and the chopped cherries. Pour this mixture over the chocolate layers and chill until firm. Top with Crème Chantilly and sweet chocolate shavings, if desired.

TIP   *If this is a dessert-to-go, take the Crème Chantilly and chocolate along and finish the pie at the last minute.*

Vanilla-Sugar

$\mathbf{Y}$es, there is such a thing, and it does make a difference in recipes. If you'd like to see what I mean, make Crème Chantilly (page 43) with confectioners' sugar and the addition of vanilla extract, then try it using 2 tablespoons Vanilla-Sugar to 2 cups cream. The difference will be immediately apparent.

Though you can buy it ready-made (see Sources, page 185), it's far easier and less expensive to make your own. Add one whole vanilla bean to a box of confectioners' sugar and seal tightly.

Within one to three weeks, depending on the potency of the bean, the sugar will be flavored.

Use it to sprinkle on cakes, cookies, pancakes, waffles, doughnuts—it's marvelous on French toast!—wherever you'd use confectioners' sugar.

If you find yourself using the sugar with some degree of frequency, you might want to transfer what's left of the Vanilla-Sugar to a large airtight jar and add up to two pounds more sugar. As you use the sugar, replenish the jar. Once a month or every other month, depending on frequency of use, pop in another vanilla bean. When the jar gets too crowded with beans, use the old beans to flavor your coffee and start over.

VARIATION

Granulated Vanilla-Sugar   *Although nowhere near as versatile as confectioners', it's delicious in cocoa and cappuccino and in your everyday cup of coffee! Follow the instructions for making Vanilla-Sugar, allowing more time for the flavor to "take."*

TIP   *If you haven't premade Vanilla-Sugar, you can make a satisfactory substitute by combining 2 teaspoons vanilla to ½ cup granulated sugar for use in recipes. However, don't use it for sprinkling and dusting; use plain sugar.*

French Breakfast Puffs

Delicious muffins on their own, these are even better when rolled in Vanilla-Sugar. If you really want to make a splash, serve with White Chocolate Butter (page 152).

Makes 1 dozen

⅓ cup combined butter and
shortening, at room temperature
½ cup granulated sugar
1 egg, beaten
½ cup milk
1 teaspoon vanilla
1½ cups all-purpose flour, stirred,
scooped, and leveled

1½ teaspoons baking powder
¼ to ½ teaspoon nutmeg
½ teaspoon salt
⅓ cup butter, melted
Vanilla-Sugar (either confectioners' or
granulated) (page 141)

Preheat the oven to 350°F. Grease muffin pans or use paper liners.

Combine the butter mixture, ½ cup of the sugar, and the egg thoroughly. Combine the milk and vanilla. Stir the flour, baking powder, nutmeg, and salt into the sugar mixture alternately with the milk-vanilla mixture. Fill the muffin tins two-thirds full. Bake for 20 to 25 minutes or until the muffin tops are golden brown and a tester comes out clean. Remove from the oven. Roll the tops in the melted butter immediately and then into the Vanilla-Sugar. Serve hot.

VARIATION
Combine 1 teaspoon cinnamon with 3 teaspoons Vanilla-Sugar for a different topping.

TIP   *Because you have to handle these while still warm, you might want to consider lining the tins with paper cups instead of foil.*

Ritva's Cake with Almonds

I never tasted anything that my sister's friend Ritva made that wasn't delicious. She had a real talent. This recipe my sister was able to get for me, and I shall forever be grateful.

Serves 8

2 eggs
1 cup granulated sugar
4 tablespoons butter, melted and
    cooled until cold
1 cup cake flour, stirred, scooped,
    and leveled
½ teaspoon vanilla
Slivered almonds
Vanilla-Sugar (page 141)

Preheat the oven to 375°F. Grease an 8-inch round cake pan.

In the small bowl of an electric mixer, beat the eggs with the sugar until almost white. Add the butter, flour, and vanilla. Pour into the cake pan. Cover the top of the cake with slivered almonds. Bake for 25 minutes. Cool 5 minutes in the pan, then turn out onto a rack to finish cooling. Before serving, sprinkle with Vanilla-Sugar.

TIP   *The best way to sprinkle sugar evenly is by using a sieve.*

Vanilla Pretzels with Simple Sugar Syrup

These are pretzels in shape only. The finished cookie is crispy on the outside, soft and delicate on the inside. They freeze well.

Makes 3 to 4 dozen depending on size

1 cup butter, at room temperature
2 cups confectioners' sugar, stirred, scooped, and leveled
3 large eggs
2 egg yolks
3 cups all-purpose flour, stirred, scooped, and leveled
1 teaspoon vanilla
Simple Sugar Syrup (below)

Preheat the oven to 350°F. Cream the butter; add the sugar gradually and beat well until the mixture is light and fluffy. Add the eggs and egg yolks one by one, beating thoroughly after each addition. Add the flour ½ cup at a time. You will be surprised to discover how easily the butter and eggs accept all that flour. Add the vanilla. Put the mixture in a pastry tube and pipe out pretzel shapes on an ungreased pastry sheet (mine look like a capital *J* in script). You may place them close together, as the cookies will not spread. Bake 10 to 15 minutes or until the tops are golden brown. Let cool for several minutes before removing from the pan with a spatula. Place on a rack to complete cooling. Brush each pretzel with Simple Sugar Syrup, then sift on plain or Vanilla-Sugar. You can also spread with White Fondant Icing (page 184).

SIMPLE SUGAR SYRUP

This can be used also to sweeten iced tea or unsweetened drink mixes. It saves a lot of stirring.

Makes ¾ cup

1 cup granulated sugar ⅓ cup water

Dissolve the sugar in the water, stirring constantly until the gritty sound ceases. Bring it to a boil without stirring (you may need to skim the scum); cook until a candy thermometer registers 225°F. Remove from the heat and let cool until lukewarm (about 110°F). Pour, without scraping the pan, into a clean jar and store until needed. If the syrup should crystallize, simply reheat until liquefied.

White Chocolate

White chocolate isn't chocolate; there's not a speck of chocolate in it, and to add insult to injury, what gives white chocolate its taste is the *vanilla* in it. The best white chocolate is imported from Europe and contains large amounts of cocoa butter. American varieties contain less cocoa butter and are better suited to cooking than eating out of hand. There is, however, one domestic manufacturer, Van Leer, in Trenton, New Jersey, who makes true eating-quality white chocolate. And at a reasonable price.

If you can't find that, buy foreign. If you can't afford that, boost the taste of the white stuff you use by adding more of its essential flavoring: vanilla.

My method of melting white chocolate in the microwave: Place in a microwaveproof glass bowl. Cook on high for 1 minute. It won't look melted but upon stirring it will soften. If you can't stir out the lumps, microwave 30 seconds more on high. You can repeat the procedure for 30 seconds more if absolutely necessary. Don't microwave more than 90 seconds total. If you use imported white chocolate and microwave it, it will not melt as quickly as the American variety. Do not microwave once you've added water to it—it will burn!

Frozen White Chocolate Mousse

This looks more like French vanilla ice cream than a white chocolate mousse, but one bite and you'll tell the difference. Unlike a frozen soufflé, this is made the classic way, without gelatin, and it has a softer texture.

Serves 6

4 egg whites
8 ounces white chocolate
¼ cup milk
3 egg yolks

¼ cup granulated sugar
1 teaspoon vanilla (or to taste)
    (optional)

Whip the egg whites to stiff peaks. Set aside. Melt the white chocolate and milk in the top of a double boiler or in the microwave. Let cool while you beat the egg yolks with the sugar until light colored and thick. Gradually pour the hot white chocolate mixture into the egg yolks and sugar. Continue beating until the mixture is cool. Taste and correct the flavoring if not vanilla-y enough. Lighten the yolk mixture by stirring in one good-size spoonful of egg whites. Fold in the rest of the whites thoroughly so no large lumps of white show. Pour into a 1-quart mold and freeze.

Quick 'n' Easy White Chocolate Mousse

It's simple and delicious—especially when made with imported white chocolate. You can make this well ahead of time and refrigerate until you're ready to serve.

Serves 6 to 8

7 ounces white chocolate
4 tablespoons hot water
1 teaspoon vanilla, preferably
   Tahitian (or to taste) (optional)

2 cups heavy cream
½ cup lump-free confectioners' sugar,
   stirred, spooned, and leveled

Melt the white chocolate in the top of a double boiler or in the microwave. Add the hot water to obtain a smooth paste. Strain if necessary. Taste and correct the flavoring if not vanilla-y enough. Let cool completely.

Beat the heavy cream until thick. Add the sugar and continue beating until soft peaks form.

Stir a large spoonful of whipped cream into the white chocolate to lighten it, then fold in the balance of the cream. Spoon into a greased 8½-by-4⅜-

by-2½-inch loaf pan, a 4-cup mold, or individual serving dishes. Chill and serve very cold.

TIP   *To make sure your confectioners' sugar is lump-free, you can sift it, or pour into a plastic bag and break up any lumps with your fingers.*

S'More Cookies

Once upon a time there was a truly talented cook who would rarely share her recipes. I don't know how my mother wormed this one out of her, but I wish we'd obtained more.

Makes 16 pieces

½ cup butter, at room temperature
¾ cup granulated sugar
1 large egg
1½ teaspoons vanilla
1½ cups cake flour, stirred, spooned, and leveled

1 teaspoon baking powder
1 teaspoon salt
6 ounces white chocolate, chopped
One 10½-ounce package mini-marshmallows

Preheat the oven to 350°F. Grease a 9-by-9-inch pan.

In the large bowl of an electric mixer, cream the butter, sugar, egg, and vanilla until light and fluffy. Add the dry ingredients and beat at low speed until well mixed. Spread half the mixture in the bottom of the pan. Press the white chocolate into the batter, then sprinkle with the marshmallows. Drop the remaining dough by teaspoonfuls over the marshmallows and spread the best you can. Bake 30 minutes.

TIP   *Once you've dropped the dough by teaspoonfuls, use your hands to spread and pat in place. The teaspoon won't do it.*

VARIATIONS
You can substitute butterscotch, chocolate, or mint-chocolate chips for the white chocolate.

White Chocolate Butter

This turns plain old bread and butter into something special.

Makes 1 gorgeous cup

7 ounces cooking-quality white
chocolate
½ cup hot water
1 to 2 teaspoons vanilla, preferably
Tahitian (or to taste)

2 cups heavy cream
½ cup lump-free confectioners' sugar,
stirred, spooned, and leveled

Melt the white chocolate in the top of a double boiler or in the microwave. Add the hot water to obtain a smooth, rather thin paste. Add the vanilla and let cool to room temperature.

With an electric mixer, beat the heavy cream until thick. Add the sugar, and continue beating until very thick. Fold the white chocolate into the whipped cream and refrigerate until cold, preferably overnight. The mixture may seem gritty, but don't worry.

Pour off any water that may have settled beneath the mixture and place the solids in a food processor bowl. Process until the mixture breaks up into large lumps. (It will look awful.) Place the solids in a strainer (cheesecloth-lined is nice but not necessary), and let sit for 5 minutes or until the excess water has drained off. Work the mixture with your hands over the strainer (more milky water will appear) until it comes together into butter. Pack into a small loaf pan (don't sweat the extra water). Refrigerate until used.

TIP *Be sure to chill anything that processes the cream: the mixing bowl, the beaters, the food processor bowl, and even the processor steel blade.*

White Chocolate Cheesecake

This is the type of cheesecake they sell by the pound, it's that dense and rich. If you use cooking-quality white chocolate, use the larger amount of vanilla. The result will be a subtly flavored dessert that will have guests guessing as to its basic flavor. If, however, you want to splurge and use eating-quality white chocolate, you can use less vanilla.

Makes 10 to 12 slivers of servings

2 cups (approximately 50) finely ground vanilla wafers
½ cup butter, melted
1 tablespoon granulated sugar (preferably Vanilla-Sugar, page 141)
2 pounds cream cheese, at room temperature
½ cup butter, preferably unsalted, at room temperature
4 large eggs, at room temperature
10 ounces white chocolate, melted
1½ to 2 tablespoons vanilla, to taste
⅛ teaspoon salt (omit if using salted butter)

If you grind the wafers in a food processor, add the melted butter and sugar and process until well blended; otherwise, mix the first three ingredients well in a bowl. Using a small plastic sandwich bag as a glove, press the wafer mixture into the bottom and partway up the sides of an ungreased 10-inch springform pan. Chill the crust for several hours, or freeze for 30 to 45 minutes.

Preheat the oven to 300°F. Combine the cream cheese and butter in the large bowl of an electric mixer and beat until smooth. Add the eggs one at a time, blending well after each addition, being sure to scrape down the sides of the bowl. Add the white chocolate, vanilla, and salt and beat 1 to 2 minutes at medium speed. Turn the mixture into the prepared crust.

Bake for 50 to 55 minutes, or until the cake has risen slightly, turned a pale golden color, and just set (there should be a soft spot about the size of a quarter in the very center). Turn the oven off and, without opening the door, allow the cheesecake to stand until cool, at least 2 hours. The cake will settle somewhat. Refrigerate for 12 hours or overnight. Serve plain or with a dollop of whipped cream or raspberry puree.

Secret Ingredients

Once upon a time, there was a woman who was such a fabulous cook that no one else could duplicate her kitchen magic—not even by using her recipes. That was because the cook, to protect her reputation, had extracted from each recipe a key ingredient that she wrote in a little skinny book. The rest of the recipe she copied into a big fat book from which she allowed her friends to copy freely.

One night her house caught on fire. As she and her husband stood watching everything they owned go up in flames, he suddenly exclaimed, "Your recipes!" and dashed into the burning house. Many anxious minutes later, he emerged, victoriously waving a scorched book in his hand—a very thick, very useless book.

The moral of the story? Don't keep your ingredients a secret. Taking my own advice, I present you with recipes which all contain one extra-special ingredient that few would guess is present.

Coconut-Crusted
Pudding Pie

You may just find this is the easiest pie you've ever made from "scratch."

Serves 6 to 8

2 tablespoons butter, at room temperature

2½ cups (1 7-ounce package) moist shredded coconut

1 cup strong hot black coffee

One 3.4-ounce package instant vanilla pudding

2 cups cold milk

½ teaspoon vanilla, preferably Tahitian

½ cup butterscotch or chocolate chips, M&M's, or Reese's Pieces

½ cup chopped toasted almonds (optional; if using, replace the vanilla with ½ teaspoon almond extract)

Preheat the oven to 350°F. Coat a 9-inch pie plate with the butter.

Soak the coconut in the coffee for about 5 minutes, stirring once or twice. Drain well, squeezing out and discarding the coffee. Place the coconut between paper towels and pat well to remove the excess moisture. Spread the coconut inside the pie plate, covering the sides up to the top edge. Bake for 10 minutes or until golden brown. Cool thoroughly.

Add the pudding to the milk. Beat about 1 minute or until the pudding begins to thicken. Stir in the flavoring. You can add the chips and almonds, if desired, to the pudding before pouring it into the crust, or sprinkle them on top. Chill well before serving. This is so rich, you might find adding a dollop of whipped cream simply gilding the lily. On the other hand, it does add a nice finishing touch.

TIP   *If using an electric mixer to make the pudding, run it on the lowest possible speed to avoid froth, which prevents a smooth top.*

VARIATIONS
Any other flavor of instant pudding may be used. Substitute 1/2 cup cold black coffee for 1/2 cup of the milk.

Cream Cake, Dream Cake!

Talk about melt in your mouth! This cake seems about as substantial as cotton candy; yet each mouthful has a clean, barely sweet vanilla taste. You know it's rich, but it doesn't taste like it. And the most difficult part of the recipe is measuring out the ingredients.

Serves 8 to 10

30 marshmallows
1 cup milk
2½ cups (approximately 60)
  ground vanilla wafers

1 cup chopped pecans
1 teaspoon vanilla, preferably
  Tahitian
2 cups whipping cream

Microwave the marshmallows in the milk in a 2-quart microwaveproof dish on HIGH for 2½ minutes. Stir vigorously, then continue cooking in 30-second increments, stirring well after each, for a total of about 4 minutes or until marshmallows are completely melted. You can also cook the marshmallows, stirring occasionally, in the top of a double boiler; it will take about 20 minutes. Let cool.

If you ground the wafers in the food processor, add the pecans and process until well blended. Otherwise, mix well. Spread three-quarters of the wafer mixture in the bottom of an ungreased 10-inch springform pan.

When the marshmallow mixture is cool, add the vanilla. Whip cream until it holds a peak but hasn't become stiff. While continuing to beat, slowly pour in the marshmallow mixture. Pour the mixture into the prepared springform pan and sprinkle the remaining crumbs on top. Chill overnight. Carefully, cut around the sides of the cake to free it from the pan. Unmold and serve cold. An obvious accompaniment would be a garnishing of sliced peaches or strawberries.

TIP   *Remember, microwaved food continues to cook after the oven goes off, so don't be in a hurry to stir after the buzzer goes off. The marshmallows will continue to melt and be easier to stir.*

VARIATION
Chocolate Cake   *Add ¼ cup cocoa to the marshmallow-milk mixture before microwaving. Substitute walnuts for the pecans.*

Easy Brownies

Okay, so it isn't *exactly* the real thing, but the ease of preparation makes up for any deficiencies. And I've never had any complaints.

Makes 20 to 25 brownies

One 14-ounce can sweetened condensed milk
1¾ cups (approximately 40) finely ground vanilla wafers

One 8-ounce package semisweet chocolate morsels
½ cup chopped walnuts (optional)

Preheat the oven to 350°F. Grease and flour an 8-inch square pan.

Mix the milk, wafers, morsels, and optional nuts. Pour into the pan and bake for 30 minutes. Cut into squares while still warm and remove from the pan.

TIP   *For a chewier brownie, bake at 325°F for 40 minutes.*

Four-Layer Pudding Cake

I first had this dessert at my husband's fortieth high school reunion. It's a make-ahead dessert to take anywhere—with pride! The many flavors and layers meld together so delectably and undetectably, you'll have everybody trying to guess what's in it.

Serves 12 generously, 18 more frugally

FIRST LAYER

2 cups all-purpose flour, stirred, scooped, and leveled

1 cup butter, at room temperature
1 cup chopped walnuts or almonds

Preheat the oven to 350°F. With an electric mixer or spoon, combine the flour, butter, and nuts, and press into the bottom of a greased 9-by-13-inch pan. Bake for 25 minutes. Cool in the pan on a rack.

SECOND LAYER

8 ounces cream cheese, at room temperature and creamed
1 cup confectioners' sugar
1 teaspoon vanilla

9 ounces (¾ of a 12-ounce container) of whipped topping, balance reserved for Layer #4

(cont.)

Blend all the ingredients together (don't overmix) and spread on the cooled baked layer. Chill.

THIRD LAYER

Two 3.4-ounce packages vanilla
  instant pudding or 1 package
  vanilla and 1 chocolate

3 cups cold milk
2 teaspoons vanilla

Add the pudding to the milk and beat at low speed for a minute or two, then add the vanilla. Chill for 5 minutes to allow it to thicken, then spread over the second layer. Refrigerate until ready to finish the cake.

FOURTH LAYER

3 ounces (reserved) whipped topping
½ cup chopped walnuts or almonds
Flaked coconut (optional)

Coarsely grated chocolate or toffee
  candy bars (optional)

An hour or so before serving, spread the balance of the whipped topping on the cold cake. Sprinkle with the chopped nuts. Add, if you wish, a sprinkling of coconut and/or grated candy bars.

TIP   *To gussy this up for truly spectacular occasions, instead of making in a rectangular pan, use a glass trifle or composed salad bowl.*

Sherry Cake

There is a restaurant in Philadelphia that's famous for its sherry cake; this is better. This cake should disappear like ice cream on a hot summer day, but if you should have any cake left over, use it to make a Tipsy Parson (page 170).

Serves 8

One box yellow cake mix
One 3.4-ounce package instant
  vanilla pudding
¾ cup vegetable oil

¾ cup cream or dry sherry
5 large or extra-large eggs
1¼ cups confectioners' sugar, stirred,
  spooned, and leveled

Preheat the oven to 350°F. Grease and flour a 10-inch tube pan.

Mix the cake mix, pudding, oil, and ¼ cup of the sherry in the large bowl of an electric mixer until well blended. With the mixer running on medium speed, add the eggs, one at a time, beating well after each addition. Pour the batter into the pan. Bake for 40 minutes or until a tester comes out clean.

Meanwhile, prepare the topping. Mix the remaining ½ cup sherry and ¾ cup of the confectioners' sugar together until the sugar is dissolved. While the cake is still hot and in the pan, slowly pour half of this mixture onto the cake. Let the cake cool for 15 minutes while you add the remaining ½ cup sugar to the topping mixture; mix well. Turn the cake out onto a rack-topped plate and spoon on the glaze, continuing with any excess that runs down onto the plate. When completely cool, take a tablespoon of confectioners' sugar and dust it over the top.

TIP *Spoon the glaze onto the cake through a fine-meshed strainer. This has two advantages: If there are lumps in the glaze, they're strained out, and the glaze flows so slowly through the strainer, you can better control its dispersal.*

Svenska "Strudel"

A truly buttery pastry, especially tender and flaky if you make it with lard. People will think the strudel is nut-filled, but you'll know better.

Makes 4 coffee cakes

PASTRY

1 package active dry yeast
1 cup milk or light cream, scalded
    and cooled to lukewarm
3 cups all-purpose flour, stirred,
    scooped, and leveled
1 cup cake flour, stirred, spooned,
    and leveled

¼ cup granulated sugar
½ teaspoon salt
¾ cup butter and ¼ cup lard or ½ cup
    butter and ½ cup margarine
2 eggs, lightly beaten

Sprinkle the yeast over the milk; stir to dissolve. Mix flours, sugar, and salt in a large bowl. Cut in the butter and lard with a pastry blender or two knives until the mixture is crumbly. Add the yeast mixture and eggs; stir to mix. Cover the bowl with plastic wrap. Refrigerate overnight or up to 48 hours.

FILLING

3½ cups coarsely crushed vanilla
    wafers (approximately 84)
1 cup melted butter or margarine
1 teaspoon vanilla

½ teaspoon almond extract (optional)
1 tablespoon water
Vanilla Milk Glaze (below)

Combine the wafers with the butter, flavoring(s), and water. Set aside.

(*cont.*)

ASSEMBLY

Divide the dough into quarters. Roll each piece into a 15-by-11-inch rectangle on a floured surface. Sprinkle with a quarter of the filling mixture. Roll up jelly roll–style from the long side. Place on a greased baking sheet and shape into a crescent. Use a scissors to make ¾-inch snips every inch around the outside edge of each crescent. Cover and let rise in a warm place until doubled, about 3 hours.

Preheat the oven to 375°F. Bake the crescents for 20 minutes or until golden brown. Remove from the baking sheets; cool on racks. If you wish, drizzle with Vanilla Milk Glaze while still warm.

The strudel keeps well in the refrigerator and freezes beautifully.

VANILLA MILK GLAZE

4 cups sifted Vanilla-Sugar (page 141) or 4 cups sifted confectioners' sugar plus 2 teaspoons vanilla

2 tablespoons butter, at room temperature

4 tablespoons milk

Mix until smooth.

S'Wonderful Ice Box Cake

Want to know where to find this recipe in my mother's recipe box? Not under *Ice Box* or *Cake*, but under *Wonderful*.

Serves 8 to 10

1 cup butter, at room temperature
1 cup granulated sugar
4 eggs

2½ cups crushed vanilla wafers
(approximately 60)

Butter a 9-by-5-inch loaf pan and line with plastic wrap or buttered wax paper.

Cream the butter and sugar. Add the eggs, one by one, beating after each addition. Beat the mixture for 20 to 30 minutes on high until the mixture increases dramatically in volume.

Fill the bottom of the pan with half of the crushed wafers. Pour the egg-butter-sugar mixture on top, and cover with the rest of the wafers. Press down to hold in place. Put in the refrigerator to chill for several hours or overnight. Remove from the pan and invert onto a serving plate.

TIP *You can weight the cake if you want, but don't go too heavy or you'll break down the egg mixture.*

Tipsy Parson

Back in the days when hard spirits were not indulged in by gentle folk (i.e., ladies and ministers), sipping sherry was considered acceptable on special occasions. Too heavy a hand with the sherry in this trifle-like dessert and the result might well be a slightly tipsy parson.

Serves 10

Two 3.4-ounce packages instant vanilla or French vanilla pudding
4 cups milk
1 tablespoon vanilla
1 recipe Pound Cake, (page 62), sliced
One 10-ounce jar strawberry jelly, jam, or preserves

½ to 1 cup sherry (cream if you have it, dry is acceptable)
½ cup coarsely chopped vanilla wafers (optional)
Whipped cream (optional)

Make the pudding in the large bowl of an electric mixer, beating in the milk and vanilla, and continue beating until the mixture begins to thicken.

Fill the entire bottom of a large clear glass bowl with one-third of the sliced cake, spread with a thin layer of jelly. Sprinkle with enough sherry to saturate the cake. Layer on one-third of the pudding. Repeat the entire process twice more, ending with the pudding. Chill. Garnish with chopped vanilla wafers or with rosettes of sweetened whipped cream.

TIP *Soften the jelly in the microwave to make it more spreadable. Don't completely cover the cake layer with it—the sherry can't penetrate to get at the cake.*

VARIATION
Strawberry jelly is the traditional filling, but also try seedless raspberry or currant jelly.
You can also add a layer of well-drained fruit cocktail or other canned fruit between the jelly and the pudding.

Triple-Decker Bars

Vanilla here, vanilla there, vanilla everywhere in these bars. However, if you prefer your vanilla sandwiched, Oreo-style, between layers of chocolate, I can arrange that, too. (If you were to ask me my favorite recipe, this would be in the top five!)

Makes 64 bars

THE BOTTOM LAYER

1 cup butter
½ cup granulated sugar
2 eggs, beaten slightly
4 cups (approximately 100)
   ground vanilla wafers

2 cups shredded coconut
1 cup chopped walnuts
1 tablespoon vanilla

Melt the butter in a large saucepan over medium-high heat. Add the sugar and eggs and cook, stirring constantly, until the mixture thickens and looks like custard.

In the large bowl of an electric mixer, blend the wafers, coconut, nuts, and vanilla. Add the butter mixture and blend well. Pack evenly into two 8- or 9-inch square pans. Chill.

THE MIDDLE LAYER

1 cup butter, at room temperature
2 teaspoons vanilla
One 3.4-ounce package instant
   vanilla pudding

¾ cup cold milk
4 cups lump-free confectioners' sugar

Cream the butter and vanilla. Add the vanilla pudding, half of the milk, and all the sugar. Add more of the milk as needed to bring it to the consistency of a thick frosting. Spread the mixture over the base in each pan and chill for at least 30 minutes or until the filling hardens.

THE TOP LAYER

Two 8-ounce packages butterscotch
  chips
6 ounces white chocolate, coarsely
  chopped (optional)

2 tablespoons shortening

While you are preparing the top layer, place the pans in the freezer. Melt the butterscotch in the microwave, using the technique described on page 115. In a clean, dry bowl or measuring cup, do the same to the white chocolate, if using. Let the butterscotch cool for a few minutes, and stir in the shortening. Using a plastic spatula, spread on top of the hardened filling. Dribble the white chocolate in a random pattern on top of the butterscotch. Score the top of the bar—going through the butterscotch layer —into 1-inch squares and refrigerate. Serve either chilled or at room temperature.

This recipe can be halved.

(*cont.*)

TIPS   *If it would make you more comfortable, use a double boiler to cook the butter-sugar-eggs. By the way, if the eggs start to scramble, don't fret, just beat well with a hand-held electric mixer.*

When microwaving morsels, always stir with a wooden or plastic spoon— the cold of a metal spoon can make the chips grainy.

VARIATION

Oh My Oreos   *To the base mixture, add ½ cup unsweetened cocoa and eliminate the coconut for a brownielike bottom. On top, use semisweet chips instead of butterscotch ones. But remember, chocolate gets hotter than butter- scotch, so be sure to let the chocolate cool for several minutes, stirring occa- sionally, before spreading on top.*

Icings and Fillings

Next to ice cream, icings must be the most common use of vanilla. The vanilla cuts the sugary sweetness of these rich concoctions, and at the same time, its ability to harmonize with other ingredients allows it to complement the cake it adorns.

Cream Cheese Frosting

Makes enough to cover the top and sides of a 2-layer, 9-inch cake or a 9-inch tube cake

One 3-ounce package cream cheese, at room temperature
1 tablespoon butter, at room temperature

1 teaspoon vanilla or Vanilla-Rum (page 133)
Approximately 2 cups lump-free confectioners' sugar

Beat the cream cheese, butter, and vanilla until smooth and fluffy. Gradually add the sugar, beating at medium speed. Do not add so much sugar that the icing becomes too thick and heavy and overly sweet.

Fluffy White Icing

A seven-minute icing, if you do it in a saucepan directly on a burner and use a hand-held electric mixer. It will take longer if done in a double boiler.

Makes enough to cover the top and sides of a 2-layer, 9-inch cake or a 9-inch tube cake

2 egg whites
¾ cup granulated sugar
½ cup light corn syrup
2 tablespoons water

¼ teaspoon cream of tartar
¼ teaspoon salt
1 teaspoon vanilla

Combine all the ingredients but the vanilla in the top of a double boiler. Place over rapidly boiling water, beating with a hand-held electric mixer or a rotary beater until the mixture stands in peaks. Remove from the heat and add the vanilla. Continue beating until the icing is thick enough to spread.

VARIATIONS

Marshmallow *Add 1 cup cut-up marshmallows or 1 cup marshmallow cream to the icing after removing the pan from the boiling water.*

Javanilla *Add 1½ teaspoons leftover black coffee to the egg white mixture before cooking.*

Lady Baltimore Cake Filling

A very unusual cake filling. It's more a fudge than what we normally think of as a filling. Traditionally, this went between the layers of the Lady Baltimore Cake (page 50). If you pour it into a greased pan, you have a delicious vanilla fudge.

1 cup granulated sugar	2 tablespoons butter
1 cup walnut pieces	1 teaspoon light corn syrup
½ cup water	1 teaspoon vanilla

Put everything but the vanilla in a 1½-quart saucepan. Stir constantly with a wooden spoon until the sugar is dissolved. Cook without stirring until the mixture thickens slightly and barely makes a soft ball (about 234°–238°F. on a candy thermometer) when ½ teaspoon is dropped into ice-cold water. Remove from the heat. Add the vanilla and beat gently until lukewarm (110°F.). Immediately apply to the cake. If the filling gets too thick, add several drops of warm water.

One-Minute Buttercream Frosting

This frosting will free you forever from buying expensive premade canned frostings. It literally takes one minute from the time you put the refrigerator-cold butter in the microwave to soften until you begin to apply the finished buttercream to the cake. The secret, of course, is the food processor.

Makes enough to cover the top and sides of a 2-layer 9-inch cake or a 9-inch tube cake

½ cup butter, at room temperature
1 teaspoon vanilla
Pinch of salt (optional if you use
    salted butter)

2½ cups confectioners' sugar, stirred,
    spooned, and leveled
¼ cup whipping cream

If the butter comes directly from the refrigerator, soften in the microwave on HIGH for 20 seconds. Place in the large bowl of a food processor; add the vanilla, salt, and sugar. Begin processing, then pour the whipping cream in through the feed tube. Process approximately 30 seconds or until the frosting clings to the sides of the bowl. This makes a soft, workable frosting. If you like yours stiffer, add up to 1 cup more confectioners' sugar.

TIP *To frost a cake without messing up the plate, take 4 pieces of wax paper and cover the perimeter of the serving plate. After you've finished frosting the cake, gently pull the wax paper out from under the cake.*

VARIATIONS

Chocolate Buttercream *Add 4 tablespoons cocoa to the initial batch. Reduce the vanilla to ½ teaspoon.*

Mocha Buttercream *Add 1 teaspoon or more instant freeze-dried coffee granules to the chocolate recipe.*

Javanilla Buttercream *Add ½ teaspoon instant freeze-dried coffee granules to the basic vanilla recipe.*

Orange Buttercream *Substitute orange juice for the whipping cream, reduce the vanilla to ½ teaspoon, and add 2 teaspoons grated orange zest.*

Raspberry Sauce

A very versatile sauce to be used with ice cream, with pound cake, or with Oeufs à la Neige (page 59). It is one of those sauces that should be in every cook's repertoire.

One 10-ounce package frozen
   raspberries
¼ cup granulated sugar

2 tablespoons cornstarch
1 to 2 tablespoons Chambord or
   orange liqueur (optional)

Thaw and drain the raspberries, reserving the juice. Put the raspberries through a sieve and discard the seeds. Mix the sugar and cornstarch in a 1-quart saucepan; stir in 1¼ cups juice (plus water if needed to make 1¼ cups) and the raspberries. Bring to a boil over medium heat, stirring constantly. Boil for 1 minute. Remove from the heat and let cool a few minutes before adding the liqueur.

TIP   *If you want only the flavor of the liqueur and not the alcohol, add it to the syrup just before removing from the heat.*

Summer Buttercream Frosting

This is the frosting of choice for the Lady Baltimore Cake (page 50). What is remarkable about it is not just its richness but its phenomenal staying power, even if the cake is kept at room temperature.

Makes enough frosting to completely cover a 3-layer cake

1½ cups butter, at room temperature
3 large egg whites, at room temperature

1 cup superfine sugar
1 teaspoon vanilla

Cream the butter thoroughly and set aside. Beat the egg whites until stiff but not dry, then add the superfine sugar, a tablespoon at a time. When all the sugar has been added, continue beating until the mixture is glossy and no longer grainy; it may take 5 minutes or more. Add the butter a large spoonful at a time, blending well after each addition. Add the vanilla.

Vanilla Glaze

Rather than using a frosting, many cooks prefer to substitute a less sugary glaze, particularly with loaf cakes or muffins.

HEAVY

4 cups sifted Vanilla-Sugar (page 141) or 4 cups sifted confectioners' sugar plus 1½ teaspoons vanilla

2 tablespoons butter, at room temperature

4 tablespoons milk

Combine all the ingredients and mix until smooth. If you mix in a food processor, you don't have to sift the sugar but should decrease the amount to 3½ cups.

LIGHT

2 cups sifted Vanilla-Sugar (page 141) or 2 cups confectioners' sugar plus 1 teaspoon vanilla

¼ cup water

Mix the ingredients together until smooth. Again, if you mix in a food processor, you don't have to sift the sugar but should decrease the amount to 1¾ cups.

White Fondant Icing

Smooth this icing carefully and it will harden into a smooth, glazed finish on which it's easy to write "Happy Birthday."

Makes enough to cover the top and sides of a 2-layer 9-inch cake or a 9-inch tube cake.

6 tablespoons butter (do not use margarine)
2 tablespoons heavy cream

One 1-pound package minus ½ cup lump-free confectioners' sugar
1 teaspoon vanilla

Melt the butter in the top of a double boiler; add the cream and sugar and beat well. Cook for 5 minutes. Cool and beat until it will spread. Add the vanilla. Thin with more cream or thicken with the reserved powdered sugar.

TIP   *When in a hurry, I don't bother to cook this icing. I just soften the butter in the microwave, add the sugar, cream, and vanilla, and frost.*

Sources

In alphabetical order, allow me to present my sources for not only vanilla but other cooking needs as well. One of the nice things about dealing with this group is that frequently you can speak to the proprietors and get answers to your questions. (You may also be subjected to their prejudices, but that can be a learning experience as well.)

Bickford Flavors

282 South Main Street
Akron, OH 44308
800-283-8322
216-762-4666

In business for almost a hundred years, Bickford makes all kinds of flavors. They have four vanillas. Bickford Natural is made from Bourbon-Madagascar vanilla beans. It is made through a special cold-extraction process and contains 35 percent alcohol by volume. The other three Bickford vanillas are made with food-grade (as opposed to chemical-grade) propylene glycol, not alcohol. Imitation (Brown) is made with artificial flavors, but contains no added alcohol, sugar, or salt as does Imitation (Clear), which has no caramel coloring. Bickford's Vanilla-Nut is clear and contains natural flavors. Offers a free price list and accepts mail orders, but, as of this writing, no credit cards.

Chef's Pantry

P.O. Box 3
Post Mills, VT 05058
800-666-9940
802-785-2198

Murray Burk is the owner and he sells his vanilla beans—Bourbon-Madagascar—by the bundle, in quantities of six or twelve, at really reasonable prices. He also offers his own label extract, including a double-strength. He carries an essence in a sugar base rather than an alcohol base for those seeking to avoid alcohol. It's perfect for making Crème Chantilly. For a catalog, send $1 which will be applied against your first order. Accepts phone and mail orders, MC and VISA.

Cook Flavoring Company

3319 Pacific Avenue
Tacoma, WA 98408
206-472-1361

Ken Cook founded this company in 1982 out of a need he saw from his ice cream business: a lack of top-quality vanillas for the home cook. He now has them, including a vanilla powder. The price list is free, but for $2 he'll send you a selection of recipes using not only vanilla but the other extracts he offers. Accepts mail orders, but no credit cards.

La Cuisine

323 Cameron Street
Alexandria, VA 22314
800-521-1176
703-836-4435

Home not only of Tahitian vanilla beans (which they'll sell by the individual bean) and top-quality extracts in various sizes, but also of that marvelous French essence I mentioned earlier (see page 22). Not only that, Nancy Pollard offers a wide selection of other essences and hard-to-find cooking supplies and equipment. Call for prices. Once on their mailing list, you'll also receive "The Cook's Advocate," their updated catalog newsletter. Send $3 for a catalog. Accepts phone and mail orders, MC and VISA.

Maid of Scandinavia

3244 Raleigh Avenue
Minneapolis, MN 55416
800-328-6722
800-851-1121 (in MN)

Candy-makers and bakers swear by this source. They say if the Maid doesn't carry it, it isn't available. Send $1 for a catalog. Accepts phone and mail orders, DISCOVER, MC, and VISA.

Nielsen-Massey

28392 N. Ballard Drive
Lake Forest, IL 60045-4507
800-525-7873

This is actually a wholesaler, but if you call, they will give you a source for their products in your area. They're worth tracking down because whenever taste tests of vanillas are done, Nielsen-Massey brands rate right at the top. They are expensive but worth it.

The Spice House

P.O. Box 1633
Milwaukee, WI 53201
414-768-8799

The Penzey family runs this organization, and they offer the largest selection of vanilla beans that I've found: Tahitian, Bourbon-Madagascar, Mexican, and a French Polynesian bean on which you can actually see the *givre* or crystalline vanillin. They also have extracts in double and single strengths. One of their nice customs is to put a whole vanilla bean in every bottle of extract they sell. Once you've used up the vanilla, you can put the bean to work. Bill Penzey suggests adding it to a quart of milk for milk shakes and vanilla floats. A delicious idea! For an illustrated catalog, send $1. Accepts phone and mail orders, MC and VISA.

Vanilla Saffron Imports

949 Valencia Street
San Francisco, CA 94110
415-648-8990
FAX: 415-648-2240

This is essentially a restaurant supplier, but they will fill orders from home cooks. They offer a money-saving 1-quart size of pure vanilla extract, special double-layered vanillas that have 25 percent less alcohol in them, so that they actually cost less than single strengths, and vacuum-packed vanilla beans. But no Tahitian beans here; Juan dismisses them as "heliotropic cheap substitutes" for the real thing.

Oven Temperature Equivalencies

DESCRIPTION	° FAHRENHEIT	° CELSIUS
Cool	200	90
Very slow	250	120
Slow	300–325	150–160
Moderately slow	325–350	160–180
Moderate	350–375	190–200
Hot	400–450	200–230
Very hot	450–500	230–260

Liquid and Dry Measure Equivalencies

CUSTOMARY	METRIC	CUSTOMARY	METRIC
1/4 teaspoon	1.25 milliliters	1 cup	240 milliliters
1/2 teaspoon	2.5 milliliters	1 pint (2 cups)	480 milliliters
1 teaspoon	5 milliliters	1 quart	960 milliliters
1 tablespoon	15 milliliters	(4 cups, 32 ounces)	(.96 liter)
1 fluid ounce	30 milliliters	1 gallon (4 quarts)	3.84 liters
1/4 cup	60 milliliters	1 ounce (by weight)	28 grams
1/3 cup	80 milliliters	1/4 pound	114 grams
1/2 cup	120 milliliters	(4 ounces)	
		1 pound (16 ounces)	454 grams
		2.2 pounds	1000 grams
			(1 kilogram)